MEMOIRS AND CONFESSIONS FROM EUROPE TO THE USA

MEMOIRS AND CONFESSIONS FROM EUROPE TO THE USA

Heidi Rhymer

Writers Club Press

San Jose New York Lincoln Shanghai

MEMOIRS and CONFESSIONS FROM EUROPE TO THE USA

Writers Club Press
an imprint of iUniverse.com, Inc.

For information address:
iUniverse.com, Inc.
5220 S 16th, Ste. 200
Lincoln, NE 68512
www.iuniverse.com

ISBN: 0-595-18130-9

Printed in the United States of America

DEDICATION

To all my family, you mean the world to me. Without your words of encouragement, and sometimes your criticisms, my story would never have become a reality.

To the many people who have played such an integral and intriguing role in my life, thank you for being there…through the good, the bad, and the sometimes ugly.

ACKNOWLEDGEMENTS

To my son-in-law for giving me a tool to write with, my computer, I am forever indebted. To my daughter, who taught me how to use this tool, thank you so very much. The knowledge you both have given me will remain forever invaluable. And especially to Beverly for all of her knowledge in editing, the person who brought my words to life. Thank you to you all!

ONE

Many years ago, seventy-one to be exact, an infant girl was born to a good and wonderful couple in Austria. The child, cherished dearly by her parents, Joseph and Maria Mueller, was named Monika. She was a beautiful little baby who touched the hearts of all those around her.

Three years later, a baby brother whom her parents named Johann (Johnny) joined Monika. Mom and Dad were so very happy. They had now created the perfect, well-rounded family they had always dreamed of.

As so often happens, time went by quickly and the children grew bigger. Now of age, Monika started school. In the pre-war days of Europe there were no buses or forms of mass transit to allow for transportation for the children to and from school, so they had to walk. It took one hour to get to school and an equal amount of time to return home at the end of the day when school was out. Winters in Austria were sometimes very harsh with enormous amounts of snow and brutal icy winds blowing off the Austrian Alps.

On walks home from school, Monika and Johnny would occasionally lie in the snow and make snow angels, all too often getting soaking wet. Thank God for the heavy coats and warm hand-knitted clothing which protected them from the cold. Surely that was why they didn't get sick very often.

Monika was eleven years old when leukemia claimed the life of her beloved father. After Daddy's death, Mama, Johnny and Monika became a very close family. Mama said, "It's just the three of us now and we have to look out for one another and make the best of it."

Daddy was missed so very much, especially by Monika. She missed and yearned for the walks they would take in the woods. He would tell her about the different trees and flowers as she wondered in amazement at what Mother Nature had to offer. She remembered that every year, as the snow started to melt, her father and she would go down to the river searching for a flower called the snow rose to see if it had begun peeking through the ground. Once in bloom, the snow rose had a very delicate blossom with a yellow center. Discovering the blossom, her father would always remark that spring was not too far away.

Monika was a straight A student. Johnny was smart but didn't grasp the lessons taught at school as easily as Monika. Time went on and Monika graduated from high school and attended Business College. Soon after, she began working for a Hatter, who is someone that makes hats. It was through this employment that she was able to earn enough money to pay for her college fees. Money had become very scarce since Daddy's death.

Tragedy struck our country! The war started and bombs were falling all around us with primary targets in the big cities. People were being injured and worse yet killed, as bombs and artillery fire hit them. I recall one particular event etched in my mind forever. The warning sirens, which we had now become accustomed to, went off but it was too late to find a bomb shelter. My employer, her sister and I went to the steel-doored cellar located below their living quarters. The building, a five-story house, was hit by the bomb. There were ten of us in the cellar with very little food, certainly not enough to feed ten people. Using our resources, we divided it equally and ate very slowly not knowing when or even if we would be rescued. Finally we were found and, after two days of digging, we were freed from what could easily have been our final resting-place. I was only sixteen years old at the time but it has left an impression on me for life, an experience I shall never forget. After we were all safely out of the building we formed a circle and offered a prayer of thanks that no one was hurt and we were all still alive and, for the moment, safe.

Workers began to look through the rubble to find any personal belongings. My boss had a little fox terrier dog and since no animals were allowed in the cellar she had put his bed and food in a hallway closet. While clearing the rubble and debris, we heard a faint whimper coming from the direction of the closet. Upon closer inspection, we found little Schatzy who was still alive after ten days with hardly any food or water. The closet had indeed been the safest place for him.

The house was so badly damaged it was not safe to stay there any longer so I moved back home with Mama and Johnny. Thankfully the war was soon over.

Austria was divided into four sectors: American, British, French and Russian. We lived in the American sector where the Enns River divided us from the Russian troops. As expected, the American troops moved into my hometown. Fortunately, my English was pretty good because it was a mandatory subject in high school. We were taught the British style of speaking since my teacher was from England. When the American soldiers would convey important things with the people in our town, my girlfriend, Elka, and I would be called on to translate. This was really more of a treat because we could put our knowledge to good use, to say nothing of how much we enjoyed the task and how important it made us feel. It also was exciting to be invited to parties that were given by the Burgermeister (mayor) and the American colonel who was in charge of the US troops in our town.

On one occasion I remember dancing a waltz with a Captain. He told me that some of his relatives came from Europe and they waltzed at home. My girlfriends' parents had a gramophone, a type of phonograph that you had to crank by hand and my mother, who was so light on her feet, would teach us to dance the elegant Vienna Waltz.

Captain Willie and I became a frequent twosome and attended all the formal affairs and functions together. He was so handsome with blond hair and blue-green eyes, to say nothing of his charm. I would be seventeen soon and had never been with a man before. One night when Captain Willie took me home from the dance with the moonlight so bright and the stars twinkling in the sky, I also had stars in my eyes realizing our hearts were so full of love. He asked me if I wanted to come to his hotel room and I willingly accepted the invitation. I knew what was going to happen but I loved him and he told me that he loved me too. We made love that magical night. Willie was so gentle and treated me with such loving tenderness that I wasn't sorry nor did I ever regret one moment of that unforgettable evening.

From that night on we were inseparable. Every free moment Willie had we spent together either going for walks along the river or horseback riding or just sitting in my mother's gazebo holding hands, being tantalized by the tuft of the lilac bush and the fragrance of the roses and peonies. Captain Willie was even talking about taking me to America as his wife. He was my first love and we cared for each other so very deeply.

One evening he came to the house with sadness on his face. He told me that his company was being transferred. He would have to leave. He didn't know when or where he was going but it would be within the week. His company left and he promised me that he would come back. Weeks went by but no word from Willie.

One very hot and smoldering Sunday afternoon my girl friend, Elka and I went down to the river to go swimming. Soon my brother, Johnny, came running down breathless and shouting, "Monika, come quickly! Willie is at the house!" Johnny and I both went running home and Willie met us halfway. What a welcome I got when he hugged me and kissed me over and over again. He wouldn't let me go. I was so very happy.

He told me that he had been promoted to major and was in Salzburg, a city about two hours away by train. He told me he had come to get me and wanted me to come live with him. We would get a small apartment and fill out the necessary papers and submit them so that we could be married. What wonderful words I was hearing and I was willing to go with him, but my mother was visiting a sick friend in the next town and I couldn't just leave without telling her. Willie assured me that he understood, but he had to go right away promising to be back the following Sunday. He gave me more hugs and kisses before he got into the car with the parting words, "Monika, I love you and I'll see you next Sunday."

TWO

I couldn't wait for Sunday to arrive and thankfully, my mother shared in my excitement. She knew we were so in love and wanted for my happiness, too.

Sunday came and I waited and waited, but Willie didn't show up. A week had passed with no word from him. Then two more weeks went by and still nothing. I just couldn't figure out what could have happened. I was so unhappy and sad, wondering if he had broken his promise to me. Were all those words just lies? Yet that didn't suit his personality. He had always been such an up front and honest person.

I told Mama that I was going to Salzburg the following day to see if I could locate him. I knew it might be a wild goose chase because I had no leads to go on. I didn't even know what company he was with but my mind was made up and I went anyway.

I was sitting on a park bench eating an apple and minding my own business when I heard someone say, "Hello." Although he was wearing civilian clothes he spoke English and, from his accent, I could tell that he was an American. He asked me if I was from Salzburg and I told him no, that I was here to look for someone very dear to me. He suggested I tell him about it and maybe he could help. As it turned out, he worked for the Provost Marshals office as a lawyer and he knew a lot of people, but he did not know Willie.

He told me that I spoke English very well and asked if I would like a job as an interpreter. I replied that I was flattered by the offer of employment however, I wasn't that good. Debating the proposition though, since I needed the money, I told him I would give it a try with no obligation. He said okay and finally introduced himself as Lt. Tony Parker. He told me he would see me the following day in his office at the courthouse.

It was a nice job but very difficult for me to understand and interpret the terms of the law. I worked with Tony for three weeks but I was a nervous wreck so I turned in my resignation. Tony assured me that he understood, but would miss me and my wonderful smile.

Six weeks had passed and I still didn't know anything about Willie so I decided that I might as well go back home. Just as I was getting ready to pack my suitcase Tony came looking for me. He said that he had some news but it wasn't good. He told me that about eight weeks before there had been a fatal car accident outside of Salzberg involving an American Major traveling to Enns to pick up his girlfriend so that they could be married. The Major had serious head injuries and never came out of the coma before he died. His name was Willie. I started crying hysterically and Tony comforted me saying that at least now I knew what had happened. I agreed, knowing now that Willie had not lied to me. He had tried to keep his promise but wound up paying with his life. Tony said the Major must have really cared.

I told Tony there was nothing left for me in Salzburg so I went back home to Mama and Johnny. I told my mother what I had found out and what had happened and she replied, "Monika, it just wasn't meant to be." That wasn't much comfort. I had a broken heart. My first love had ended in such horrible tragedy.

I began searching for another job but didn't know exactly what I was looking for. There weren't very many jobs available unless you had some type of experience. All I knew was how to make hats. One day I was having dinner at a restaurant, sitting by myself, when a waiter came up to me. The place was very crowded and no other tables were available so he asked if I would mind sharing mine. I said of course not since I would be leaving soon. The man he seated across from me appeared to be in his late thirties and he introduced himself as Felix. We started talking and he told me that he was looking for a partner for his act. My curiosity peeked so I asked him what he did for a living. He told me that he owned a small circus, but during the winter they performed at clubs and theaters. He mentioned that his partner had gotten pregnant and had to quit her job. Now he was desperately looking for someone to take her place. He informed me that I was about her size and asked if, by any chance, I was looking for work? I replied that I was but didn't know exactly what I was looking for. He then asked if I would be interested in performing with him. Naturally, I wanted to know what I would have to do. He said his act was divided into three parts and lasted about twenty minutes or so. The first was a cowboy act where he would twirl a lasso in small loops and then bigger ones eventually roping me into the ring. The second part was a thin rolled sheet of paper, which I held in my mouth as he cut it off with his whip. In the third segment I would stand with my back against a board as he threw knives outlining my body. That sounded scary but he said he had been doing this for a while and never missed. I retorted that there was always a first time!

It, none the less, sounded very intriguing! I had never done anything like that and was willing to try anything once. I told him I didn't want to be obligated if I didn't like it and he agreed. He told me that he had a performance the following Saturday and I needed to get acquainted with the act and also to try on the costumes which might need a tuck here and there. He also mentioned that if we went out of town a hotel room would be provided for me and that the pay was very good. I told my mama and her advice was that if that was what I wanted then I should give it my best try.

Our first performance was at the American Officer's Club. I was so nervous I was sure that the audience saw me shaking. My cowgirl outfit was really beautiful and consisted of white leather boots, a very short white skirt with frills at the bottom, a silver blouse and a white hat with a silver hatband. That was just one outfit and I must say they all looked fabulous on me. Even Felix said it matched my personality and how very proud he was of me.

After our performance we were permitted to mingle with the people unless we had another engagement at a different club and had to leave immediately after the show. I enjoyed the time that I worked with Felix. He was so very nice and was also very appreciative, especially when I had done a good job for him.

Spring was almost here and the performers regrouped and started practicing their new acts so they would be ready when the circus went on the road. Felix asked me if I wanted to stay with them but I declined because I didn't want to live the life of a vagabond. Every so often when I heard the circus was in town I would stop by and talk with Felix. He was always glad to see me remembering how well we had worked together. Sometimes I would reminisce, wondering what it would have been like to be a circus performer. I know I would have seen many cities and would have met a lot of people but I guess I am just a solid ground type of person.

I started working for a family with two children, a boy and a girl named Franz and Liesel. I liked my boss and his wife a lot and they seemed like everyday sort of people. I also got along well with the children. I was like a live-in maid for them.

I went to the movies one night where I met a man named Jimmy. He was very nice and asked me out. We saw a movie and then decided to go to a club and dance for awhile. We had fun together and he was crazy about me. He also helped me get over Willie. Then, just when I thought things were going good for me, Jimmy was transferred to the United States because his tour of duty in Europe was over. I saw him one more time before he left.

One morning soon afterward I woke up feeling kind of puny and nauseated and naturally thought I was coming down with something. My condition didn't improve over the next few days so I went to the doctor. He ran all sorts of tests and to my surprise he said, "Young lady, you are going to be a mother. You're pregnant!" You could have knocked me over with a feather! I was in shock. I started crying as I told the doctor the whole story. What was I going to do now? The father of my unborn baby was gone and I had no way to contact him.

I told my boss the whole story, too. She assured me that they would see me through this. She was such a dear and kind person. I worked up until my eighth month of pregnancy then came home to Mama. My mother was kind and understanding, too. She never made me feel ashamed about the baby I was carrying. In fact, she said we would raise the baby together.

On January 17th, 1948, my baby boy was born. He was so tiny and pretty, I could hardly believe that I had brought this perfect little child into the world. I do believe his father would have been proud of him, too. I named him Walter Jimmy, reversing the first and last names of his father which, was Jimmy Walter. It sounded good to me anyway.

In the home where I was working I could not bring the child. There was just no room in their apartment, so my wonderful and beloved mama took care of little Walter. I saw him every weekend and was amazed at how fast he was growing, turning into a perfect little man. You could tell grandmother and grandson really bonded. Mama Maria gave him all the love and attention a mother could give her child; more than I could give him just on the weekends. As much as I loved him there was no way I could be with him all the time.

Everything was going well again. My boss was so wonderful and she gave me a lot of clothing that her son had outgrown. My little baby boy was dressed well and besides that Grandmother Maria sewed a lot of things for him, too.

There weren't very many things a single woman could do except go to the movies and there was one playing that I really wanted to see so I went one night. I had to transfer from one streetcar to another and wait about ten minutes for the other streetcar to arrive. There was a soldier waiting for the streetcar also and he asked me what time it was. I had a watch but it had stopped so I guessed the time to be about 8:00 p.m. He was amazed and delighted that I spoke English and that we could communicate. He asked me out the following week. I instinctively liked him so I accepted even though I could smell alcohol on him. I was thinking that maybe he'd just had dinner and a drink. In Europe it wasn't uncommon to have a drink with your meal. He told me he would meet me in front of the Coliseum Movie Theater and I agreed.

I remembered that he was very tall, older than me and very nice looking, handsome, in fact. His name was Carl J. Bridges. Our meeting was at 7:00 p.m. and we arrived almost at the same time. When he saw me he greeted me with a handshake. He was wearing his uniform and I could see that he was a Sergeant.

After the movie he suggested we do it again. The next time we went dancing at a club. Carl wasn't a very good dancer so he didn't mind if someone else asked me to dance as long as he had the first and last dance with me. Carl did have a beautiful voice and he didn't mind at all singing country and western songs with the band. The people just loved to hear him sing all the old tunes like "Carolina Moon" or "My Happiness". He was nice and very intelligent but I found out that he had a problem. He drank too much. At first I thought it was the people buying him drinks for singing some requested songs. But that wasn't it. He was from North Carolina where moonshine whiskey was made in the mountains and he had been at it for many years. I doubt if he could ever give it up because he just didn't have the will power.

Even with his problem, I really liked being with him. I also liked to sing, but not on the stage like he did. I was much too timid and would get flustered. We did get along beautifully.

Carl was renting a room from an opera singer and his family near the Kaserne (base) where he was stationed. After the war money was very scarce and many families would rent out rooms to soldiers for some extra income. Carl asked me to quit my job and move in with him. I had to think about it very seriously because of his drinking but, in the end, agreed in hopes that he might slow down. I quit my job and we set up housekeeping.

As we got to know each other I found out he was from a city in the Smokey Mountains of North Carolina where the people are nicknamed Tarheels. I really don't know the meaning of that. I also found out that he was divorced and had six children. He told me that he knew five of the children were his, but the sixth one, his wife had confessed, might be someone else's child. Therefore, they were divorced. Clearly, he was older than I was…seventeen years to be exact.

I, in turn, told him about myself and that I had a little boy, not omitting the circumstances of how he came to be. I told him that my mother was taking care of him and she loved him like her very own child. At this point, I thought if Carl thought anything of me he would suggest that little Walter come and live with us. That dream never happened.

I got pregnant by Carl and on July 6th, 1949, a beautiful little girl said hello to the world. She was my joy beyond compare. Carl also loved the child with all his heart. We named her after both of her grandmothers, Millie Maria.

Carl had asked me to marry him, but again I was very hesitant because of his drinking. I found out that he not only drank on the weekends, but that he liked to also during the week after he got off from work. I was so depressed; I just didn't know what to do. If I married him and he drank all the time that wouldn't be any life for Millie and me. Yet if I didn't I would have another fatherless child, only this time it was different because he did want to give the child his name. I agreed to be his wife in hopes that everything would work itself out. So we were married.

THREE

We submitted our marriage papers and had interviews with the Chaplain and the Company Commander. They both talked with us very sincerely because of our age difference and also about the role of an Army wife. Sometimes husbands would be with their families, and then twenty-four hours later they would be fighting a war. We took what they said under consideration, but decided we really wanted to get married.

We were married on the 3rd of September, Labor Day. We had no church wedding but never the less it was very beautiful. A Justice of the Peace performed the ceremony. I wore a cream colored, ankle length dress with silver and gold designs. I also wore a short veil with a headband that had tiny wax flowers and petals on it. Everybody thought that was really unique. I also wore three-inch heels since Carl was six foot two inches tall and I was only five foot three.

The reception was fantastic and all our friends were there including Mama and Walter and the company commander and his wife. The reception lasted until about 10:00 p.m. Mama and Walter left earlier since they had to take the bus back home and Millie was taken care of by our landlord who really loved her.

We had a one-night honeymoon since my new husband had to report back the next day to his company. Married life was wonderful and Carl even slowed down on his drinking, but of course it didn't last. We would have arguments every time I mentioned anything about my son, Walter. Carl would say, "I'm not raising some other man's child." I cried a lot over those words many, many times.

Not too long after Carl and I were married, we took a trip by train to Vienna. After arriving there we found out that over night the script money that the soldiers got paid with in Europe had changed. So there we were with only the old script money we had arrived with. To our luck, we found out that at the train station there was an office for the American soldiers and civilians stationed in Austria. Fortunately, it was there that we could convert the old script money for new currency. Had it not been for a young couple we happened upon we would not have known where to go. Because the change took everyone by surprise, the lines were very long, but we finally managed to make our exchange.

Eric and Lillie, the couple who had directed us there, offered to show us around Vienna since we were unfamiliar with the surroundings and we gladly accepted. Carl and I got a hotel room and freshened up, then we met Eric and Lillie in the hotel lobby. It was such a beautiful day, Lillie suggested that we go swimming. Luckily we had brought along our swimwear, so off we went on the trolley car. In my youth I knew my way around Vienna somewhat but since the war, everything had been rebuilt, so we were grateful to our newfound friends for their assistance in guiding us. We rode quite a while before finally arriving at the swimming area. It was a huge facility with all the amenities. We lounged by the pool, sipping beer for almost the entire afternoon. That evening Carl and I invited them to join us for dinner in reciprocation of their kindness.

We met again the following day to see some of the highlights of Vienna. Eric and Lillie took us to Schonbrunn, where we saw the Palace of Maria Teresia, once the Empress of Austria. We viewed the many monuments of Goethe and other famous composers, too. A bit tired, Eric and Lillie invited Carl and me to their apartment. I noticed, as did Carl, that it was very empty. There was a magazine rack with many Polish and Russian newspapers, which we found a bit curious. After having a drink, we then went to the restaurant. This time, they picked up the tab. It was yet another wonderful ending to a perfect day. We made sure to take an abundance of photographs to show our friends at home. Alas, as the old saying goes, 'time flies when you're having fun'. It was time to leave.

Once at home, we had our film rolls developed and showed the snap shots of our three-day vacation to our friends. One of them pointed out to us that we had gone swimming in the Russian Sector, which really gave us a fright because we were caring a camera and Carl was in uniform. The law was at that time, no American soldier was permitted in that sector, especially with a camera and wearing a uniform. Why no one stopped us or said anything to us will always be a mystery, a mystery that will never be solved. It then crossed our minds that perhaps Eric and Lillie could have been spies and that was why we were never stopped or questioned. Talking about the incident later sent shivers down our spines. We could have gone to jail for violating the rules. The bottom line, however, was that we had a wonderful time and the pictures to prove it. Tremendous as it was, I will always wonder why Eric and Lillie chose us to be our guides.

One day Carl was drinking very heavily and I really thought he was going to hit me so I packed a few things for Millie and me and we went to Mama's for a visit. It was then that my wonderful mother said, "Monika, I want to adopt Walter. I love him like my own child and eventually you will follow Carl to America. I surely wouldn't want that little boy to be where he isn't wanted. Besides that, he would be wonderful company for me." It broke my heart to think I would move so far away and never see my son again.

As autumn arrived Carl became very ill. He had an infection in both lungs and had double pneumonia. He was admitted to the base hospital and there was even talk that he might be shipped back to the States since his tour of duty was almost up in Europe. This became the final decision and he was transported, with medical assistance, to a hospital in New Jersey.

It seems drinking always got Carl in trouble. One day he would be a Sergeant and a few weeks later he would be demoted to Corporal because of some incident. He was just climbing the ladder first up and then down again.

Millie and I had to wait for my passport and visa, which would take a few weeks before we could leave. Finally I got notice of my port call which was just days before Christmas. We had to take the Orient Express train to Bremerhaven, Germany, and from there board a ship to New York. A lieutenant brought my travel orders to me at the train station in Salzburg. Millie and I had a Pullman compartment on the train. When we weren't eating or sleeping, we would watch the cities pass by. This was all new to me, as I had never been to this part of Germany before. Time actually went by quite fast since the train did not make very many stops. It was a trying ordeal though, to be away from my mama and Walter at this special time of year, but then I remembered what the Chaplain and the company commander had told me about my new life as an army wife so I tried to be strong.

On that trip many memories would come popping in my mind. The holidays were always so special to us, especially Christmas. Mama and Dad would go all out to insure that we always had a wonderful Christmas. I remember we would get nothing sweet a month before the holidays so that we would really appreciate what we got from Santa Clause on Christmas Eve. Mama and Dad would always make sure the happy times stayed with us the rest of our lives so that we could also teach our children and grandchildren the meaning of Christmas and tell them the traditions of our childhood and customs of our country.

It was very hard for Mama when my brother Johnny finished school. There was no employment available. So after the war he thought perhaps going to Canada would give him a better opportunity in life. He had heard that there were many jobs available to immigrants. He left right after the New Year and since he wouldn't become eighteen until October he had to get permission from my Uncle Johann to leave. He was my mama's sister's husband and became our guardian after my father died.

Mama was truly left by herself now except for my little boy, Walter. Life works in strange ways at times but it seems that everything has a way of falling into place and turning out best for everyone. Even if my husband had agreed to raise Walter, my mama would have refused to give him up because he was her third child now.

Back on the train I was getting excited because I had never been to a port before or ever seen a big ship. I had been on a river cruise but nothing compared to this huge passenger vessel I was about to sail on across the Atlantic Ocean to my New World, my new life.

As the ship started slowly moving out onto the big waves I could still hear the band playing "Auf Wiedersehen" (till we meet again). I had learned the song as a teenager and never thought it would ever have such a special meaning to me as it did now.

We set sail on Christmas Day aboard the USS Darby. Millie and I had a cabin all to ourselves and we dined with the Captain of the ship and had our own waiter and steward. When I got acquainted with some of the other passengers I was told that they had eight to ten people in a cabin and there was barely enough room to turn around. I couldn't believe that Millie and I were so fortunate to have a cabin all to ourselves.

The days seemed to go by very quickly. We went to the movies, which Millie really enjoyed no matter what was showing. She got a little seasick but the doctor at sick bay took care of that. I played cards and cribbage with some of the passengers, games I had learned to play at the post Special Service Club. I had always been interested in learning new things and when Carl wasn't drinking too much he was a good teacher and I learned many games of entertainment.

We were high at sea and soon it would be New Year's Eve, the beginning of a brand new year for my brand new life. The Captain announced that we would have a little party to ring in the New Year and he asked me if I minded helping out. I would see to it that the punch and chip and dips were all in order, which were being prepared by the cooks. It was a privilege to be asked and I felt it appropriate since I was dining at the Captain's table. To my surprise we had a very elegant table setting. The party turned out marvelously and the Captain thanked me for putting in a few extra suggestions here and there.

We were getting closer to New York and we received our landing passes and also a message to see the Purser. I had to pay thirty-three dollars for the food and that was when the mystery was solved. My landing pass stated: Monika Bridges, wife of Colonel Carl J. Bridges! Instead of corporal they had written Colonel and now I knew why we had the special privileges. This was just one of many experiences to remember.

The ship docked in New York at 9:30 a.m. on January 3rd and my husband was there to greet us wearing a military police badge. When the other passengers saw us hugging and kissing they didn't know what to think.

The error was obviously made in Austria when they were typing it out. We also were booked into the St. George Hotel, which was strictly a transfer point for officers. I was awed at seeing New York City, which I only knew from movies and magazines. We arrived at the St. George Hotel and what a place that was. I couldn't believe that a subway train was running right underneath the hotel. The room was beautiful and there were even services available. All we had to do was dial a number if we needed a babysitter for Millie. She was very tired so we called the sitter and decided we would go out and look around, exploring the sites of the city. Carl and I went downstairs and stopped at the St. George bar and had a few beers. I tried different beers but liked Pabst Blue Ribbon the best.

In the morning we were going to ride the subway. I sure had never seen trains like this before. We were going to see some of the highlights of New York. We got our tokens and waited for the train. When it arrived I got on first and waited for Carl and Millie to board, but the doors closed automatically. I was on the train and Millie and Carl were outside! Carl called to me shouting, "Get off at the next stop!" It was sheer panic for me. I had no idea that the train had no conductor like they have in other cities, but then this was not an ordinary train either. It was running underground. I got off when it stopped next and waited for Carl and Millie. It took seven minutes before they arrived and I was still trembling when I saw them. He explained a lot of things to me after that which made me feel better.

Together we went to 42nd Street and I just stood there with my mouth wide opened wondering at all the lights and decorations that were still up from Christmas. To me it looked like I was in a fairytale. We stopped at Macy's department store and I saw some moving steps. Carl told me that they were called escalators so I just had to try them out. What a wonderful invention I thought. Shoppers could get around a lot faster this way.

One experience I will never forget is the hat Carl bought me. It was pretty cold out and we had seen a 'sale' sign. I didn't know what that meant but I learned fast that items were marked down to half price. On the table was a black straw hat and Carl bought it for me. I told him that in Austria we wore felt hats in the winter and straw hats in the summer but he said it looked good on me so I wore it the entire time. I was so proud of that hat! It was my first purchase in New York and for that matter, my first purchase in America.

Carl mentioned Chinatown and, of course, again I had no idea what that was, but he explained. We stopped at a bar and restaurant because Millie was getting hungry. In fact we all were, so we ate and had a beer. Naturally, it was Pabst Blue Ribbon. Carl was very proud of me and he mentioned to some people that I had just arrived from Austria the day before. A gentleman in his fifties overheard the conversation and talked to us for a little while then he asked us not to leave until he came back. We had no idea why but we agreed to wait. In about thirty minutes he returned with a beautiful long stemmed red rose in his hand. He gave it to me and said, "Welcome to America!" I had tears in my eyes as I thanked him and he gave me a hug. I thought people in America are just so friendly and nice. He gave me his business card and said if I was ever in New York again to be sure and give him a call. He would love to hear what I thought of this great country of ours.

We stayed three days at the St. George then we took the train and went to New Jersey where Carl picked up his leave orders. From there we continued on to North Carolina. On the way we saw such beautiful country with mountains that sure reminded me of Austria. We were going to Ashville, N.C. and then by bus to Waynesville where Carl's parents lived.

It was all so exciting but at the same time scary too, not knowing what the family would think of me since Carl's oldest son, Carl Jr., was only nine years younger than I. We arrived in Waynesville and took a taxi to the house. Here was my mother-in-law and father-in-law hugging and kissing Millie and me, worried that I might not be able to understand them. The compliments came again on how well I spoke English.

Carl's folks were the kindest and sweetest people. I got along with them really well. I even hit it off with Carl's children. In the back of my mind I was thinking so much about Carl having these kids by a different woman but yet he didn't want mine. At any rate, we all got along well and they thought of me as a friend, not as their stepmother.

I have always been an honest person and yet I found myself sneaking around by sending my son some small gifts in the mail. Mama had sent me some photographs of Walter. He was so handsome and growing up so fast. How proud I would have been to have my son with me, too.

FOUR

We only stayed one week in North Carolina before Carl had to report to Ft. Belvoir, Virginia for his new assignment. We stayed in Ft. Belvoir from January to May then Carl got orders back to Europe. I loved Ft. Belvoir and we had nice quarters only thirty minutes away from our nation's capital, Washington D.C. I remember one time some of my new found American friends informed me that I was going to go with them to D.C. It was George Washington's Birthday and everything was on sale at the stores. If I hadn't seen it with my own eyes I would have never believed it. People were standing in line all night and day even sleeping on mattresses on the sidewalk so they would be there first when the stores opened on February 22nd. We looked in some stores but didn't find any bargains. They were already sold out. I did buy a green patent leather purse with a shoulder strap that I liked very much.

This was just another wonderful experience I had on my first trip to the United States. We had many opportunities to go sightseeing and we took advantage of them, but now Carl had his orders and this time we were going to France.

In order to go back with my husband I had to become an American citizen but one had to be in the United States between two and five years. Carl said, "Let's go to D.C. and find out what can be done." So we did. We met a Mr. James Palmer who handed me a book that was not very thick and told me to study it and come back in one week. I had to also bring two witnesses that I had known for at least one year. I studied the book and Carl quizzed me on the questions so that I would answer them to the best of my ability. We took Millie to North Carolina so I could have more time to study and memorize all the questions. One week later it was time to see Mr. Palmer. I brought two witnesses, one that I knew from Austria and her husband who was stationed in Austria at one time. The other was a neighbor that had known me since we'd moved into military quarters.

We met Mr. Palmer and he said to come with him. I followed him and he asked how I was doing? I replied that I was very nervous but I had read the book that he had given me. I was so surprised when he only asked me three questions. The first one was "What do we celebrate on the 4th of July?" I answered, "Independence Day." The second one was "How many Senators from each state are there?" I replied, "Two." And the third question was "Who is the Vice President now, under President Truman?" When I answered Albert William Barkley he said that I had done very well and asked if I also read and wrote in English. I told him fifty-fifty, and he said that he believed me. I had to sign some papers and so did my character witnesses and then he told me that he would inform me when they had the naturalization ceremony. They swear in one hundred people at the same time. I told him that I would be looking forward to hearing from him. My husband had already gone to France so I stayed with my in-laws until I heard from Mr. Palmer.

I enjoyed staying there and learned so much from them. My mother-in-law was a terrific cook and she showed me how to make cornbread, biscuits and sawmill gravy, which is what they called white milk gravy. Cornbread was something I wasn't used to. At home we would feed corn to our chickens and pigs and use the silk from the ears to make hair for our dolls. It was a real treat to learn how to make bread from ground up corn.

My father-in-law was a Baptist minister and would preach evenings at the church sometimes. He was really great and could bring the word of God to all the people, leaving no doubt he was a Christian. Like everybody else, he had his faults though. One morning I walked into the kitchen and saw him pouring some liquid stuff into jars. My curiosity got the better of me so I asked him what it was. He replied that he was making 'homebrew'. I was baffled, not knowing what that was. I came from a country where they drink beer like they drink tea in America but homebrew, he explained, is not as strong as regular beer yet quenches the thirst very well after it is fermented. He gave me a taste but I could honestly say that I preferred Pabst Blue Ribbon a hundred percent better.

On October 1st I received a card from Mr. Palmer telling me to be in Washington, D.C., at the Court of Justice, on the tenth of October. My stepdaughter, Ruth, went with me since she had never been to our Capital and I was honored that she wanted to be present on this very special event for me.

There were so many people there at the Court of Justice building and we had to listen closely for our names to be called then, walk up to the Justice's bench. Finally, I had heard my name so I walked up with the rest of the people and we all repeated the Oath together before the Judge. With that he announced, "You are now all American citizens." We congratulated one another then had to wait for our naturalization documents. Ruth and I had waited about two hours already and we were getting hungry. I tried to find out how much longer it would be when I saw Mr. Palmer and he said he would find out for us. When he came back he explained that he had sent the card to me personally, instead of his secretary and therefore she didn't bring my file. Mr. Palmer went to talk to the Judge but he had already left for Chicago and wouldn't be back until Friday. Mr. Palmer asked if we could stay until then so I agreed, promising that we would meet him at 10:00 a.m.

Strange but true, I was the only one repeating the Oath before the Judge and Mr. Palmer, then Ruth congratulated me on finally becoming an official American citizen. After I received my citizenship papers I had to go to the passport division and sign for my passport and visa. I also had to go to the Pentagon to get my travel orders signed and finally we were on our way back to the beautiful Carolina Mountains.

When we arrived back home Ruth told and retold the story that I had to be sworn in twice and everybody said that was because I was so special. When I think back now, the old saying stands true. I was at the right place at the right time because not too many people have the privilege of becoming a citizen of the United States in ten months. Not long after that I received my port call to go to France.

I called the lady that was my witness in Washington. She was now living in Peekskill, New York, while her husband was away on assignment and she said this would be a perfect time to visit.

We left North Carolina a few days later. When we arrived at Grand Central Station we had to board a train to Peekskill, which wasn't that far away. Marianne and her daughter, Evelyn, who was Millie's age, were waiting for us at the train depot. It sure was nice seeing them and we had a lot of catching up to do telling each other what had been going on since our last encounter.

The next morning after breakfast, Marianne took us to town and showed us what this fabulous tourist city looked like. We stopped at one place where there was a cosmetic analyst. There they matched up the color lipstick to your complexion and since I'm fair skinned I was matched with a light purple/pink which was really pretty. I had never been to a cosmetic analyst before so it was a real treat! We also had a delicious meal at a wonderful little diner. It was such a nice visit and as we parted, we promised faithfully to write to each other.

Millie and I went by ship again, this time on the USS Rose, an equally nice boat. Only this time it was the 'real' me, a Corporal's wife. We shared a cabin with two other ladies and their three children, but it was okay. We kept each other company by playing cards and some games with the children. We also went to the movies and played bingo for recreation. Of the three of us, only Millie and I went to France. The others were going to Germany.

We arrived in Metz, France, by train from Bremerhaven. Carl and two other soldiers picked us up in a staff sedan. It was about an hour's drive to where we had to go. We stopped at a French restaurant to eat and have a beer but, of course, it wasn't a Pabst Blue Ribbon but a French beer. My husband asked me if I needed to use the bathroom. I said I could wait until later. Well, I finally had to go and the guys couldn't wait to see my reaction. I walked in the door but came right back out. The men were laughing so hard when they saw my expression. I chastised them. They had told me to go to the wrong place. All I saw were two footprints and a hole in the middle of the floor. They finally stopped laughing and explained that since I had never been to France before I was not familiar with the culture and their ways of living. That was the right bathroom. After this incident if someone mentioned 'footprints' we would have a big chuckle remembering what happened on my first restaurant and restroom visit in France.

FIVE

Our four years in France was mixed...good and bad, happy and sad. One of the more memorable times was when I first learned to drive. We bought a used Air Force sedan and I thought it was the most beautiful car there was. I also thought there was nothing to driving a car. Well, I was wrong! Carl started teaching me at first but he made me so nervous. I thought I knew enough about the car and was going to show him that I could do it on my own. I started out fairly well, and did fine on the French country roads. That is, until I came to a railroad crossing one day and a train was approaching. The bars came down and I couldn't stop quickly enough. The hood of the car slid under the bars losing its' hood ornament. Needless to say, this scared the wits out of me but I believe it made me a more careful driver in years to come. Finally I mustered up enough courage to take the test for my driver's license. The road signs were in English and French, the written test in English only, which proved to my advantage. I only missed about three questions on the test and I got my driver's license.

I was so proud of my accomplishment. Now I could take Carl to work and pick him up and have the car to myself all day. I would take my friends to the commissary or Post Exchange, but the best thing was I could visit my Mama and Walter.

All three of us, Carl, Millie and I, went the first time, but when we got there Walter almost didn't know me. I hadn't seen him in over a year. He would call me Mama, but to him my mother was his real mama. In a way it made it somewhat easier when we left.

While in France I got pregnant with twins but miscarried in my fourth month of pregnancy. The doctors told me I would have never carried them full term because the placenta was beginning to attach to the uterus. It took a lot out of me, mentally and physically. I only weighed a hundred pounds. I had to rest a lot because I tired so easily. Carl started drinking more and more. It was easy to get caught up in the trap because alcohol was cheap in Europe. Carl truly was a decent person. He was a good husband and a wonderful man when he wasn't drinking, but when he had too much booze he was the devil himself. When we had fights, and believe me they were hurting fights, he would hit me for the slightest things I did or didn't do. The next day he would always tell me he was sorry, especially when he looked at me and saw the bruises on my body. He swore up and down that he would never do it again; but then there was always a next time. There were times when he wouldn't drink for a week or so, but then on weekends some of his drinking buddies would stop by for a visit or they would take us to a bar. It never was just one drink. There was always just one more for the road.

On one of his good days, he came home from work and asked if I would like to go to England and see the coronation of Queen Elizabeth the Second. I thought he had flipped out completely because nobody had a chance to do that, especially a corporal and his wife. Never the less, he had two tickets from Special Service Tours to attend the coronation.

We left by bus from Toul, where we were stationed, to Verdun France. While waiting for the bus I drank way too much coffee. Finally we boarded for the one and a half-hour drive. We were on the road about thirty minutes when I had to go to the bathroom because of all the coffee I'd consumed. I went up and told the bus driver, so he stopped by a high embankment near the road. I ran down the hill not paying attention to where I was squatting. Much to my embarrassment I was in clear view of all the people on the bus. Oh well. The grass was kind of tall so I thought it would be okay. I never noticed that there was nothing but stinging nettles in the grass and I got blisters all over my backside! Thank goodness I had some Vaseline in my travel bag which I used immediately when we arrived in Verdun. What an embarrassing thing to happen before such a fabulous event. When I told friends about the incident they couldn't help but laugh. At least they could have felt a little sorry for me.

We took a train from Verdun to Paris, then from Paris yet another train to Dieppe, where we got on a boat that crossed the English Channel. There was some bed space for people who got seasick; otherwise you had to sit at the bar or catch forty winks propped in a chair. Well, with my experience with the nettles I didn't feel like sitting so I told the boat attendant that I didn't feel well. Sure enough, I got to sleep in a bed. Carl stayed at the bar for the five hours it took to cross the channel. When we got to England we boarded another train to London. It was a very exciting, but tiresome journey. What army wife, though, could say that she went to the coronation of the reigning Queen of England?

There were so many people in the crowd that in order to take any photographs you had to hold the camera up high and hope to capture something. I got a few good pictures just to prove that I was really there. We did have one lucky break when, due to the congestion of the horse drawn carriages, the Queen's carriage stopped right in front of us and she waved. I really got a close look at her. England is famous for the rain but, lo and behold, it wasn't raining on this momentous day. I brought back some very nice souvenirs, a small replica of the Queen's carriage that she was riding in and also a replica of the Lord Nelson monument. We also brought back newspapers with headlines of the event. It was truly a memorable trip and I will always be grateful that I had the opportunity to go.

On the way back home we stopped in Paris and Carl showed me where he had been stationed before we met. He fought in the War of Normandy in the Battle of the Bulge.

Before we found a place to live in the city of Toul, we lived out in the country. We had such fun as the neighbors made wine and we helped them stomp the grapes in giant barrels. Our feet sure got discolored from the grapes but the experience was worth it. Carl loved fried oysters and I could buy them here still in the shell. The packaged ones were very expensive so I started getting the fresh ones and used my own oyster knife just to make it easier. One day I bought two dozen of them and as I opened one I found something hard and dark gray inside. I took it out but it rolled out of the palm of my hand. I searched the floor over and over yet never did find the strange object again. I asked a jeweler one time what it could have been and he explained that it could have been a black pearl, which is very rare and expensive. We didn't have a vacuum cleaner at the time so when I swept the floor I kept on looking, but the cracks were pretty deep. After that I always looked inside the oysters each time I bought them but never found another 'treasure' inside.

Finally we moved to the city of Toul and rented a two-bedroom apartment. Millie was getting bigger and we needed more room. We had a great time in Toul and Millie learned the language quicker than I did. We enrolled her in the local French school because she was too young to go to the American one. My husband played Santa Claus one Christmas for the children in Millie's class. They called him Pere Noel and from then on we became very popular with the teachers, parents and, of course, the students. We were invited to many functions and attended as many of them as often as we could.

Our new landlady was super to us. Her name was Madame LeCompte and with her broken English and my French dictionary, we understood each other perfectly. Madame LeCompte had a beautiful rose garden and grew a very dark red rose. You had to look at it twice or you thought it was black. I helped her a lot in the garden because I enjoyed it so much and she really appreciated that, too.

By now I was getting used to things like our toilet, which was an outhouse with the 'famous' footprints. There was another American couple living in the complex and we became very good friends. Pearline and Ian were from the state of Maine and to this day I still get a Christmas card each year from them. She mentions, with laughter, how Carl used to squat on the footprints reading his paper and doing his business. They have been wonderful friends throughout the years. When we were there they had no children but once they started, they couldn't seem to quit. They had nine! They named their first little girl Millie, spelled the same way as our little Millie, and all the rest of the children's names began with an 'M', too.

While in France I joined the NCO wives club and was elected Treasurer. I had no experience in things like that but my personality proved I could do anything I set my mind to. I suggested we have a raffle to make money and, even though our prizes were very inexpensive, with our selling technique we sold every ticket and made $500.00 for the organization. The club also took many short trips, by bus or car, to see some very interesting places and sights. One time we took a bus trip to Lourdes and we visited the Shrine and Grotto which are famous draws for tourists and those wishing to be healed by the Virgin of Lourdes.

There wasn't a lot to do in the wintertime so I asked if anyone would be interested in me teaching them how to knit and crochet. I didn't know a great deal about it but enough of the basics to make a sweater, scarf or socks. Everyone loved the idea and they all made warm socks and had a ball doing it.

I was also a party girl and we attended a New Year's Eve party at the home of our friends, Cora and Sam. It was bigger than ours and could hold more people. The club was forty-five minutes away so it was much safer to go somewhere local. I remembered something we used to do when growing up so I asked Carl to get a few sticks of lead to bring to the party. To do this we needed a pot of boiling water and a ladle. You melted the lead in the ladle and poured it in the boiling water. Whatever formed would be your good luck charm for the New Year. This was a hit with everyone as they were all curious as to what theirs would look like.

While stationed in France and after I learned to drive, there was no stopping me from going anywhere! Once I had figured out approximately where it was that I wanted to go I would venture out by myself. My wonderful blue Air Force sedan that we had purchased in Stuttgart, Germany was my pride and joy. When the French franc was at a low exchange, we would go to Luxembourg where you could get more for the American dollar. I recall the first time we went there with one of Carl's friends, Willie. It was a beautiful drive. We could still see barbed wire in places, all remains of the war. It was only about a four-hour drive there, which had been nicknamed Little America because you could purchase any American goods as though you were in the United States.

When we arrived in the city, we got two rooms at a hotel, one for Willie and the other for Carl and me. After dinner, as always, we found the best bars in town. There was one not too far from the hotel called "Charlie's Bar". They had two floorshows; one at ten p.m., the other at one a.m. Needless to say we stayed and enjoyed the shows. Even though it was a 'girlie' sort of entertainment, it was good. Carl and Willie wanted to stay for the one o'clock show, of course. While waiting for the second show, a twelve-piece orchestra began to play and, as usual, Carl was ready to sing with the band if they permitted it. There was one very famous song of the time called "Mariandle". Now Carl didn't know the words very well, but he did know the melody. We were having a wonderful time as another American couple joined us. Everyone urged

Carl to go up to the band and asked if he could sing a song or two. Right away the bandleader agreed. He began to belt out the lyrics to "Mariandle" and immediately got a big applause. Although he didn't know the words, everyone was yelling 'encore'. He began singing some American songs and entertained the entire bar. The time, however, was drawing near for the second show to begin.

The second show was a bit more risqué, with more revealing costumes, but never the less, it was an excellent performance. What does one expect? Luxembourg was a neighbor to France and these shows were everywhere. When the show ended, three of the entertainers came to our table and started hugging Carl, paying little attention to the females at the table. Willie was unattached, but our husbands were very much taken! That was probably the first time I really got jealous of Carl, as did Francis, the other lady who had joined us. She and I boldly stood up and informed the 'ladies', and I use that term loosely, that they were messing with our husbands! They took the hint and began to leave, but not before Carl managed to pluck a feather from one of the costumes, just as a souvenir, of course. The effects of the alcohol were beginning to hit us, so we decided to call it a night. We returned home the following day.

Now that I knew the route to Luxembourg, two of my friends and I attempted to make the trip alone. The exchange was pretty good and it did help us out in making the dollar stretch a little further. We left fairly early to insure we would be travelling by daylight. About twenty-five miles from Luxembourg, we got behind a big truck going up a hill. There was no passing zone or shoulder to pull over on. I don't have a clue what happened next. When we could finally pass the truck my car wouldn't go into third gear, so we drove the duration of the trip in second and immediately searched for a garage. Having finally found one, I was told that I had stripped a gear. They could fix it right away, but the cost was the amount of money I had come to exchange. There went all the profit I had intended to bring home. If that wasn't bad enough, I was scared to death of what Carl would have to say since I had almost all the money with me that we were supposed to live on the rest of the month. Taking pity on me, my friends paid me for taking them. Even so, that wasn't enough to make up the difference.

I was a wreck! I had no idea how Carl was going to react. Once back at home, Carl asked if we'd had a good trip. Shaky as I was, I couldn't put off the inevitable. I told him that we didn't make any kind of profit, that in fact, we didn't have any at all. I feared the yelling would begin but instead he asked what I was talking about. Crying hysterically, I proceeded to relate our misadventure to him. Was I ever surprised! He merely replied that it was okay. Mishaps can target anyone. After all, it was a used car when we got it. What a relief! I could breathe normally again. We were fortunate that it was repaired, considering it was an American automobile. In France, generally the parts have to be ordered from the States. Carl and I returned to Luxembourg just before Christmas to get Millie a doll carriage. We did a little sightseeing and visited the grave of General George S. Patton.

Our four years were up and it was time to come back to the United States. The NCO Wives Club gave me a farewell party and had a big banner stretched across the wall saying "Thank You, Monika" honoring me for everything I had done for the club. I cried and hugged everyone thanking them for the wonderful farewell party.

We took one last trip to Austria to say good-bye to Mama and Walter. It was so very hard to leave this time. Walter was in school already, but Mama said not to worry, that he would be all right, somehow knowing we would be back again soon.

Our new orders were for Presidio, California. We flew from Paris to New Jersey landing in the Azores for fuel. It was a landing strip in the middle of the ocean that belonged to Portugal. It was really beautiful with nothing but water surrounding us. We had a meal of roast beef and cabbage in the Mess Hall then flew on to Fort Dix, New Jersey.

SIX

When we arrived, we bought a brand new car, a 1955 white and turquoise Plymouth. I loved our blue sedan, but this car was a dream. We drove it cross-country, stopping off in North Carolina to see Carl's family.

A lot had happened while we were away those four years. My in-laws were still just as warm and loving to me and thought I was the finest daughter-in-law there was, but they were getting on in age. Mother Millie was seventy-five years old and Dad Oscar was eighty, both plagued with arthritis. The doctor had also discovered that my mother-in-law was diabetic. We hated leaving them, but we had to be at our new destination soon.

Driving cross-country was a real treat because I learned so much and enjoyed every minute on the road. As we traveled through the Mojave Desert I was amazed at the vast land of nothing but sand and cactus scattered throughout the region. I was even more surprised when I found out that a glass of water cost ten cents. We learned that because of the miles and miles of desert their drinking water had to be hauled in so they had to charge for this precious commodity.

While traveling in Arizona I saw many different types of cactus growing wild next to the highway, and being the plant lover that I am, I wanted to dig some up but the only thing I had was a teaspoon. I used it and dug up several plants until I was rudely interrupted by a horned toad or, as some people call them, a Gila monster. Needless to say I went back to the car in a hurry. I didn't want to meet up with another one of these creatures or anything else for that matter. I'd heard there were plenty of snakes, too!

We finally arrived at the California border and the border patrol officer asked us if we had any fruits, vegetables or plants of any kind. I opened my big mouth and said that I'd just dug up some cactus with a teaspoon. He said sarcastically that he was sure that was a lot of work, but he had to take them anyway. He cut the roots off and gave them back to me, but I knew that they would never grow that way and I sure didn't want them now. As if to comfort me, he said he had to abide by the rules and regulations. We thanked him and went on our way to San Francisco and our new assignment.

We stayed overnight in San Bernardino, a nice little city not too far from Los Angeles and Las Vegas, Nevada. Our cabin key had a little rabbit's foot on it and when we checked out the next day I asked the clerk why it was on the key chain. He told me that their customers kept it for good luck or a keepsake, so I kept ours. It brought us good luck in our travels for many years to come.

I loved California. It was a completely different environment than what I had seen so far in the United States. Everything was so expensive but I guess that was to be expected from the movie capital of the world.

We stayed in the military guesthouse at the Presidio base for a few days until we found a place to live. When Carl signed in with his company he explained to the Sergeant our situation. His name was Walt and he said we could stay with him as his wife, El, was visiting her family in Nebraska and there was plenty of room. After staying ten days at Walt's, we heard about a house that was for rent in Sausalito, a resort city across the Golden Gate Bridge. We inquired about it right away and the owner let us rent it for a price that we could afford. That rabbit's foot really brought us luck that day.

Across the street from our new home was the shore of Sausalito Bay. The backyard had two cherry trees and a fig tree and the other part was covered with artichoke vines and flowers galore. It was a wonderful house situated above an area that used to be a television repair shop. The owner had opened another store in San Francisco where he was living, so now it was empty. The den had an alcove facing the bay and it was furnished with bamboo living room furniture with flowery cushions. All we had to buy were drapes. This would be the first household item I would buy on credit. The curtains were made of a lacy material with all kinds of leaves and a few flowers to match the cushions. It really was 'me' and it made for a cheery atmosphere.

There were boat races nearly every weekend and we would sit in the den and watch them. It was so strange because in the front of the house you would have to wear a sweater because of the cool breezes, but in the back of the house you could sunbathe.

We had some wonderful neighbors next door. The Alden's were an older couple, but very friendly and they just loved Millie. When the figs got ripe I tried to sun-dry or oven-dry them but never got the hang of it so we ate them raw, right off the tree. The artichokes were something different to me but our neighbors showed me how to prepare them and to this day we still enjoy them.

Just two houses away was the corner grocery store. Carl started drinking Mogen David wine. I like a glass of wine now and then but I do believe this was the worst wine I had ever tasted. This was the beginning of trouble as Carl would drink the stuff and get tipsy a lot, which just caused us to have more and more arguments. Nothing seemed to please him.

Millie started school in Sausalito just a few blocks away from the house. I would walk with her in the morning and pick her up in the afternoons. It was good exercise for me and the wonderful smell of the sea made me feel alive.

We met a wonderful older couple, Haline and Corman. Again, another couple who thought Millie was so adorable and such a beautiful child. Haline became our baby sitter and later on when Millie was baptized in the Presbyterian faith they became her godparents.

One day I found an advertisement for a file clerk in San Francisco. I had never worked here in the United States but thought I would give it a try. So I called for an interview and got an appointment to see a Mr. McCameron who was office manager for the Fire and Indemnity Insurance Company. The home office was located in Los Angeles.

Mr. McCameron was a very handsome man with salt and pepper hair, dressed to the hilt and a smile that would melt anyone's heart. I think he liked me from the beginning because he said he would give me a try and see how I liked working for them. I learned my work very quickly and I was very grateful to have a chance to prove myself. Since it was my first job I didn't want to appear dumb but I sure was scared to death and hoped I would do a good job.

I made a lot of friends. There were about thirty employees in the office, and I got along well with all of them. They were all very helpful too, from the claims manager to the fire and car underwriters. Also the typists gave me a helping hand whenever I needed one. I even initiated a once a week bowling team. A lot of the employees signed up and we did pretty well, but we all needed some practice. Regardless, it was a lot of fun. Someone asked why no one had thought of this before.

One day I noticed Mr. McCameron watching me wrapping some office material to send to another agent. He said that I wrapped those parcels better than he did his Christmas presents. "Maybe I should hire you for that," he said and then smiled. He was really such a good man and liked by every person in the office.

One day we heard through the grapevine that he was going to get a promotion to the Los Angeles home office. The entire office was going to miss him, especially me since he had helped me so much with everything that I had learned. I had a deep respect for him.

After Mr. McCameron left, Al, one of our special insurance agents, became the new office manager. I knew Al because he had come into the office often to discuss things with Mr. McCameron. Al was a good manager, too, and since I worked closely with him we had become good friends.

One day Al invited another lady named Rosita and me out to dinner. Rosita was a fire insurance underwriter. She was divorced and had a daughter Millie's age named Patti and we had become very good friends. Al asked us if we had any preference as to where we wanted to go and I said jokingly, "How about on top of the Mark?" I had heard so much about the Mark Hopkins, one of the finest restaurants on Nob Hill. Al said, "Okay, the Mark it is." I said I was just teasing, but he insisted that we would go there. This was some place that my husband and I could never have afforded. It was lavish and high classed, so it was a big thrill for me to go. Rose said that even though she was born in San Francisco she had never been there either so it was a double treat.

What an elegant place it was! Why, they served little Vanda orchids from the champagne fountain. No wonder everybody that was anybody stayed at this fabulous landmark place. After the wonderful dinner Al asked us where else would we like to go? We really didn't care to go anywhere else so we thanked him very much for the tremendous time and told him we would see him on Monday at the office.

I had never been to Reno, Nevada to go gambling and my neighbors, the Aldens, were going to Idaho for a visit and told me that I was welcome to ride as far as Reno and then take the bus back. It's only about a three hour drive from Sausalito. I was really excited to go. Haline took care of Millie and off we went on Saturday morning. This was country I had not seen before. There were pine trees everywhere which reminded me of home in Austria.

We had dinner at a place called Cal-Neva and spent the night there. The hotel gave us a complimentary roll of nickels and while we waited for the dinner to be served that roll of nickels burned a hole in my pocket. I was so anxious to play the slot machines, having never played them before. I got up and got busy. I put in about six coins and the machine started going crazy with noises and lights flashing. I thought I had broken the darned thing, or hit a wrong button, but the attendant came over and said I had won a jackpot. I received a whole eight dollars and that's all it took to get me started playing the slots.

My husband was sent to New Foundland for five months, but came back in only three with a new set of orders. This time for Fort Devens, Massachusetts. So it was time for us to move again. I was sure going to miss my job and the wonderful friends I had made, especially Rosita. When I found out that she shared the same birthday as Millie, I began to plan parties for Millie and her friends, then in the evening I would have one with our co-workers for Rosita. It turned out very nice and we had a ball. By the time I gave my notice to quit and my household goods had been packed, almost three weeks had passed. Mr. McCameron sent me a letter of recommendation plus a very nice letter to me personally wishing me good luck in my new endeavors. He also said that if I ever came back to the Bay area and needed a job I would always be welcomed at the insurance company. The office staff gave me a going away party and everybody attended. They gave me a beautiful Samsonite make-up case and a card with everyone's signature, even Mr. McCameron's. I never did find out how they managed to get the card back from Los Angeles in time for the party. I was sad to leave because they were the nicest people in the world.

SEVEN

The trip from the West Coast to the East Coast was very long. Of course we stopped in North Carolina again as we always did when travelling, then off to New England to our new home. Carl had always said that he wanted me to see as much of the United States as possible and that was his fondest wish. I was very grateful that I had this chance. It enabled me to make so many friends along the way and over the years. By now I had been through thirty-eight states and collected a glass from each one. When we had company, if I had a glass from that person's home state, I would let them drink from it. Sometimes the glasses got broken but the people enjoyed my thoughtfulness.

We arrived in Massachusetts and I discovered yet another place to explore. We preferred to live off post and found a two-bedroom cottage on the lake. The people who owned it used it as their vacation home and rented it out between seasons. Our backyard was a mass of blueberry bushes and we could hardly wait until they ripened. We even got a little boat and painted it bright orange. Our friends donated the paint in exchange for boat rides on the lake. In shocking contrast, the oars were a vibrant red.

It was so very pretty there. Part of the lake in our cove was filled with water lilies and when in bloom they would lavish the lake with their beautiful white and yellow flowers. One time I picked some of them and filled the bath tub with water and put them in it. Carl thought I had lost my mind because we did, after all, have to use the tub to take a bath, but they looked so pretty.

The lake was full of bluegills and gars. Millie learned to fish and loved it. She didn't care to put worms on her hook though, so she used bits of cheese instead. Strangely, she did catch fish with her bait and got pretty good at it. One time she and her little friend Mellie bought some baby turtles and made a little pond by the shore for them. They lined it with sand and put a plastic cover over it for the night. The next day the turtles were gone though. I suppose they crawled out and went down to the water.

Autumn was absolutely awesome in that part of New England. The leaves turned the most beautiful yellow, orange, and rusty red colors. When they started falling off the trees we knew that winter would be making it's entrance soon.

One morning we woke up and the lawn was blanketed with almost four feet of snow. We shoveled from 7:00 a.m. to 3:00 p.m. just to get to the highway and to our mailbox. The highway had been cleared with the snowplows sent in from the city, but where we lived it was all privately owned land so we had to do it ourselves.

I had brought the snow skis I'd used as a teenager from Austria but had never been able to use them in the United States. This was a perfect opportunity to try them out. Hopefully the old saying was true. When you learn something you never forget. I did fairly well; a little wobbly at first, trying to keep my balance, but I made it just fine out to the main road. Coming back to the house, however, was a different story. I ran into the corner of a snowbank too sharply and slid around it at full speed. I was sore for several days from that tumble but didn't give up. I kept trying and finally mastered the art again.

Christmas was right around the corner and for the first time in a long while it was a white one, just like the ones we used to have in Austria. As was done every year, I mailed a package to Mama and Walter with money and some American candy that they thoroughly enjoyed. We had a beautiful Christmas tree and, although Carl was still drinking a lot, he enjoyed the holidays, too. He did his best to make things festive and invited several soldiers over to share in our festivities.

For Thanksgiving and Christmas we always had dinner at his company mess hall on post so that we could be with some of the men who were unable to go home to their families. We enjoyed those times so much and the food was always delicious. I couldn't see cooking a big ole' turkey for just the three of us, anyway.

Time seemed to go really fast after the holidays and soon spring was on it's way. We still had a few cold days, but the sun had melted all the snow. As I've said before, I love the springtime best. I think because it means a new beginning for everything that survived the harsh and bitter cold winter. The trees started budding with new leaves and birds were busy building their nests and laying their eggs. When they hatched they would join in chorus chirping a beautiful spring melody.

Just as we were enjoying this beautiful time of year, Carl got orders again. This time for Korea. Wives and children were unable to accompany their husbands and fathers on this tour. I wanted to go to Austria but we didn't have the money for the airfare. I really didn't want to stay in Massachusetts because there would be too many things to do to keep up the house and grounds and I knew I couldn't do them by myself. So I wrote to my old boss and friend, Al, to see if I could still get a job at the insurance company again. A few days later I received a telegram from Al saying they would welcome me back with open arms.

I was so glad. At least now I knew what I was going to do. I also wrote to Haline and Corman asking them to look for a small apartment for

Millie and me, preferably in Sausalito. They found a place through a friend of Halines', who was a widow and rented out the bottom floor of her house. She had converted it into a two bedroom furnished apartment. This sounded perfect and was also at a price we could afford.

Once again we were on the road going across country. We stopped in North Carolina to see Carl's family, then on to Tacoma, Washington, where Carl would take a ship to Korea. This was a completely new route for us and, of course, more new states to see. We had passed through desert and sand before but the scenery now was mountains and green lands.

We stopped at Yellowstone National Park and saw the geyser Old Faithful that erupts every seventy to eighty minutes and sprays water far up into the sky. We also saw some smaller geysers, but instead of spraying water they made the earth boil with bubbles right in front of your eyes. What an eerie feeling. I sure didn't know things like this existed in this world. They say seeing is believing and now I sure do believe that these things can come up from the ground. We also saw a black bear along the road. I wanted to take a picture of it so we stopped What I didn't know was that it was a mama bear with her cub following. She was very protective of her baby and fearing she might turn on me, I made a quick dash back into the car. I did manage to get a picture of her, but safely through my car window.

When we left Massachusetts we traded in our car for an older model to lower our car payments. What we didn't know was this car was using more oil than gasoline so our funds were depleting quite fast. We got as far as Cameron, Montana, when it became necessary for us to call Haline asking her to send us my allotment check so we could rent a log cabin. The people trusted us to stay until we got the money in the mail. It was a good feeling to know that there were such nice people in the world. Cameron is about forty miles from Butte, the state capital. Cameron, itself, was a very small town and consisted of a long building next to the highway with four cabins, a bar, post office, restaurant and a laundromat. Almost every night we would see cowboys come in from the ranches to have a few drinks. I had never seen a real cowboy in person, only in the movies. Nor had I witnessed somebody striking a match on the soles of their boot. I was so intrigued that one cowboy even gave me three long matches that I still have to this day with the name 'Cameron, Montana' on them. We had been invited to go on a hayride to Butte on Saturday but my check arrived and we had to move on. Before we left, I bought a postcard to mail to Mr. McCameron in Los Angeles. I told him I didn't know he was so famous that he had a city named almost after him. He got a big chuckle out of the card.

We traveled through Utah with it's scenic high mountains and on to Washington State to drop Carl off. Then Millie and I headed for California. When we traveled through Iowa we saw so many cornfields, but you couldn't buy any ears at the vegetable stands. While going through Washington we found a stand and I bought ten ears. Then it dawned on me that I didn't have a pot to boil them in so we left them in the trunk of the car until we got home to Sausalito, at least that is what I thought. Guess what? We got to the California border and were asked if we had any fruits, vegetables or plants. I had to tell the patrol officer I had just bought some ears of corn at a fruit stand and he told me I would have to give them up. So there went the corn that I wanted so badly, much like the cactus.

As we were traveling down the highway, Millie and I really got a scare when we saw grass burning on the side of the road. It looked so gruesome and made us wonder if we should stop and try to put the fire out. A little further down the road we saw the fire fighters and knew they were taking care of all the hot spots.

We finally made it to Sausalito where Haline, Corman and our new landlady Mattie were anxiously awaiting us. The apartment was really cute and just big enough for Millie and me. It was located on Main Street, at the other end of town from where we had lived before. It was still pretty close to the bay, about two blocks from the water's edge.

The next day I called Al and he was pleased to hear that we had made it safely. He asked when I was coming to work and I told him I needed at least a week to get settled in. That was fine with him so he would see me the following week.

Most of the old employees that I knew were still there and they really did welcome me back with open arms. Over my desk was a banner with "Welcome Back, Monika". That really made me feel good. It was so nice seeing everyone I used to work with again, especially my good friend, Rosita. Rosita was Chinese and I couldn't have asked for a better friend. It didn't take me long to get back into the routine again of being a working girl.

Haline was taking care of Millie after school and she just loved being with her and Corman. They would take her to their house and she would play by Haline's goldfish pond. Corman, of course, spoiled her rotten and she got away with everything.

Saturdays and Sundays were my time to spend with Millie. We would go to San Francisco where they had continuous movies playing and we would sometimes see three or four of them, one right after the other. After the movies we would go shopping and dine out. Sometimes on these weekends we would visit some of Millie's school friends. One of them lived right on the beach in Sausalito. It was such a beautiful place and you could tell they were pretty well off to own a mansion like that.

Rosita and her mother invited Millie and me for dinner one evening. We called Rosita's mother 'Mama Chan'. She didn't speak any English so Rosita had to be the interpreter for us. The food Mama Chan fixed was very delicious, but every time you would tell her it was good, she would come and fill up your plate again. I told Rosita that I was ready to explode. Before we left, Mama Chan gave me something although I'm not quite sure what it was. It could have been a desert or fruit but we put it in a doggy bag and took it home. It was a delightful day with a wonderful family.

Christmas was almost here and I received invitations to a lot of parties from the people I worked with. Also Al, my boss and friend, started taking Rosita and me to different places again. He didn't talk very much about his wife, but we had heard that she died of cancer. We guessed that it just made him feel better taking us out. He once said it was good for his morale. We felt special too, because he was a very good-looking man and always dressed like a movie star. He was nothing less than a perfect gentleman and we knew he could have any lady he wanted but he preferred being with us.

One day Al came up to my desk and informed me that that evening we were going to a yacht party in Sausalito. Rosita agreed to go, too. One of our special agents had his yacht docked in the bay and we would all be going. Rosita and I dressed up very elegantly because we really didn't know what to expect since neither of us had been anywhere so 'up town'. What a welcome we got! The host told Al that it was a pleasant surprise for him to bring such charming ladies. We knew a lot of people there. Rosita knew some people that I didn't because she had been with the company a lot longer than I. All in all, we sure had a terrific time. I never realized there was so much room on one of those boats since I had only seen them from the outside, but the twenty people on board were able to move about comfortably and freely.

For the holidays, I decorated our little apartment with all the Christmas flair, but it sure didn't feel the same as in the past. For one thing Carl wasn't there and the other was that it was eighty degrees outside which didn't get you much in the holiday spirit.

Time passed and soon it was spring. I believe it was in May that I experienced my first earthquake. We were all working when all of a sudden we heard a rumble and it felt like the building was swaying. Al told us it was an earthquake and to get under our desks so that we would have some protection. It was over very quickly, but out there in the heart of the city was a lot of broken glass. It was also reported that gas pipes and water mains were busted and for all people to stay away from those areas if at all possible. Some of our staff was coming back from lunch when it happened and they walked in very pale from fright. They had been in the elevator! It sure was a scary experience with no warning of any kind.

I tried to call Millie's school but the switchboard was jammed. People could call in but no one could call out. Haline did manage to reach me and told me everything was okay. No one was hurt and Millie was with her. When I got home that day I found out that Millie's school had a big crack on one side of it's wall.

Two days later we were still feeling some aftershocks. I was having lunch in the lounge when I almost fell off the chair. It was a powerful jolt and then a smaller one after that. Then it was over. The fear in everyone still lived on, to think it might happen again. That was the only earthquake I ever experienced and I hope it will be the last one in my lifetime.

Carl came back from Korea and stayed maybe two months. He then got orders for Fort Hood, Texas. I remembered traveling through that state. It took us two days just to cross it. At that time it was the largest in the United States before Alaska was made the forty-ninth state. I also recalled how very hot and dry it was. I doubted very much that I was going to like it there. I cried and was very sad when we left Sausalito, San Francisco and my wonderful friends.

EIGHT

Arriving at Fort Hood was an experience in itself. We couldn't get housing on post. We were two hundred sixty eighth on the list, so we had to stay at the guesthouse for three weeks. We couldn't even find a place to rent because there weren't any houses available. It was a very large post with lots of families.

We spent a great deal of time searching and looking for a place to live. It was just disgusting because it was hundred-degree weather and it was September. Finally, we heard about a house for sale in Copperas Cove, a small community about seven miles west of the post. We went to see about it right away. The owner, who was an Air Force Sergeant, had gotten orders for Washington and had to sell his home. He said we could have it by just taking over the payments. I sure was one happy lady now that we finally had a home of our own. It was an older house, but to me it was a castle. I kept it spotless. Carl was happy about it too, and he helped plant shrubbery and did a lot of 'honey-do's' around the house that needed fixing. We had to buy some used furniture, but didn't have enough money to accommodate the whole three-bedroom home, yet we managed pretty well.

The house was in an ideal location, just a block away from the school Millie would be attending for fifth grade, within walking distance. We didn't have a lawn mower yet so Carl persuaded some of the guys in his company to borrow the company lawn mower. Four guys showed up and helped mow the grass and, of course, we had to furnish the beer. It was a large yard, a lot and a half, but they all took turns and in no time we had a very good looking lawn.

Carl's drinking didn't slow down, and we were really in bad shape money-wise. We had to borrow money galore from credit companies, a lot of which went for booze.

We stayed in Texas for two years then Carl got orders again, this time for Germany. I had gotten used to a lot of things, even the heat, so when it was time to move on again I really hated to leave. By the same token, I was happy, too, because it meant I would get to see my son and Mama again.

We made arrangements to rent the house to a family with five children. They really loved it. For one thing the school was close by and we had a big backyard with a playhouse that Carl had built for Millie. One morning she went out to play and found a tiny rabbit. The neighbors said it might be a wild cottontail that had gotten lost from it's mama. Millie left it there and eventually it ran away, or perhaps the mama found it.

Carl's youngest son, Douglas, joined the Air Force and took his basic training in San Antonio. When training was finished he got his assignment for Alaska. He came to Copperas Cove and rode back with us to North Carolina. Before we left we showed him the local sights and the base on Fort Hood where his father was stationed. We also showed him our recreation area on Lake Belton. On the way back home we saw an armadillo resting next to the road and Douglas decided he wanted to catch it. He jumped out of the car and tried, but the critter zigzagged as he was running after it. It was an impossible feat. When he got back in the car it reminded me of one of our visits to North Carolina when Carl's family was going to show me an opossum in the hills behind my in-laws house. They were having fun with me as they told me to hold a long stick and wait till the opossum came out of it's burrow and then rattle the bushes around it. I stood there holding that stick, but never saw it. Somehow they caught it though, and put it in a gunnysack holding it by it's tail. When we got back to the house they let it go and it ran up a tree stump. I had never seen an animal like that before so naturally I had to take some pictures of it.

We left for North Carolina the following day and it sure was great having someone to help me drive. I usually did all the driving because I loved it, but when you travel cross-country like we did, it could make a person very tired at times.

After a short visit in North Carolina, we went on to New York to report to the ship. We were lucky we got to go to Germany because of the Cuban Crisis, where most of the troops from Fort Hood were headed. If that wasn't bad enough a hurricane was battering the Texas coast. Before the ship left we got to do a little sightseeing. We went to the Empire State Building and walked all around it. My feet were so sore that I could hardly move, so I pulled off my shoes and walked barefoot, right there on the streets of New York City.

This time we sailed on the USS Polk. When we left port we experienced the tail end of the hurricane that had caused so much damage to the Gulf of Mexico in Texas. We really had a rough voyage for a few days.

The cabin that was assigned to us started flooding. Water was seeping in on the floor and after only one day at sea we had to move. We got a cabin on the top floor next to four officers who apparently were making their first trip to Germany. They were studying the German language and were pretty funny and loud as we listened to them through the cabin wall. We met them the next day and played scrabble with them. I asked them if this was their first time to visit Germany and they replied that it was. They were trying to learn the essential words so they could communicate with the folks there. So I told them that I would answer them in German while we played scrabble. They were very appreciative and gave me a heart-felt thank you. As we were playing scrabble, all of a sudden the ship jolted and we skidded across to the other side of the room. The table, scrabble tiles and two guys were on the floor. Thank goodness no one was hurt. The sea was pretty rough that day.

Carl and I joined in on a lot of the ship's activities. We played canasta, pinochle, bingo and cribbage, to name a few. It really was great to join the fun and it made the time pass more quickly. Millie went to the movies a lot and also joined in on some pastimes for her age group.

After ten days at sea, we arrived in Bremerhaven, Germany. We traveled to our new destination, Munich, by train. It would be our home for the next four years. Thankfully, we got quarters immediately, but had to sign our lives away. The apartment was really nice and located on the second floor of a three-story housing complex. It had three bedrooms, a living room, dining room, kitchen and a long hallway leading to all the rooms, but it had only one bathroom.

Once again I made new friends. One especially dear and wonderful one was named Charline. She and her husband, Jackson, were from Norman, Oklahoma and live there to this day. We don't get to see each other very often but we do write and reminisce about our times in Germany. She had two sons who went to the same school as Millie. She and I did so many things together like window shopping in downtown Munich, then having dinner in a fancy restaurant and eating a big slice of those delicious German cakes. I just loved to listen to the famous Glockenspiel. It had such a unique sound. We also took some short day trips to see King Ludwig's Castles. He had several of them within an hour's drive from our home.

We also participated in Fashing, where people dress up in funny clothing, and dance in the streets, very much like Mardi Gras in New

Orleans. Charline called me one day and asked if I wanted to go downtown to see what was going on. I said sure and off we went. We put shower caps on our heads in an attempt to fit in with the crowd. We got to dance more dances that day and had a barrel of fun.

One time we visited the Botanical Gardens. This was right up my alley since unusual plants, flowers and ferns had always fascinated me. They had a pond and in it were these flat leaves twice the size of a pizza pan, that curled up at the edges and people would toss coins in to the pond. I never did find out what they were called or why the people did that other than maybe for good luck.

Millie and I went to see Mama and Walter soon after we arrived. I couldn't believe how much he had grown. He would call me Mama but I knew his 'real' mama was his beloved grandmother. I was hoping and praying that some day Carl would let Walter live with us, but that wish would never be fulfilled so I went home as often as possible. At Christmas, Carl went with us and it was a precious time for me to spend with my mama and my son, to be there on Christmas Eve, in the place where I grew up and cherished so much. After we had eaten and exchanged gifts, Mama wanted to go to midnight mass. There were ten of us total so we all piled into the car and Carl drove us to the service. He didn't want to go into the beautiful old Church because it wasn't of his faith so he waited outside for us. For all I knew he might have gone to the local bar for a few drinks. When mass was almost over and the congregation was singing "Silent Night", out of no where came this powerful voice singing the song in English. The melody echoed throughout the church and everyone turned around to see who it was. I have never been more proud of my husband than I was at that moment. I know he did it for his mother-in law. She had tears in her eyes and gave Carl a big hug. She didn't speak much English so she said "Danke schoen, my dear Carl. That was really wunderbar." As we left, there was a lot of snow on the ground and flakes were still falling. They glistened like diamonds as the headlights shone on them. Everything and everyone felt so serene. I knew at that moment there really was peace here on earth, and I believe all the others did too. We had to be back in Munich the day after Christmas but, to this day, thirty-five years later, I can still remember how we celebrated the birth of Christ on that evening.

We had many good times while in Munich. Even our good friends, Walt and El, came to visit us. They were stationed in France and drove to Munich. It was time for October Fest, which is a very big event in Munich. We drank beer and danced to the 'oompa' music. Walt and El were always very special friends from the day we met them in California until they passed away a few years ago. When they retired, they moved to Boulder City, Nevada. Every time I had a chance I would visit them and also nearby Las Vegas where I did a little gambling. El passed away first, which was such a tragic loss for me. She had been a nurse, and was a victim of that terrible disease cancer. I saw Walt three times after she died but he, too, was ill and in the hospital a lot. I think after his beloved wife passed away he just gave up and lost his will to live. They had been married for almost fifty years. One day I received a phone call from a friend of theirs and he gave me the news that Walt had passed on, also from cancer. I miss them both very much. Good friends like that are very hard to find, but the memory of their kindness when Walt invited us to stay with him at his house will always stay in my heart.

Another place we visited, this time with Jackson and Charline, was the very famous Hoffbrau Haus. We got acquainted with two gentlemen from Santa Fe, Argentina. They were in Munich to learn how to make beer and were very intelligent business people. After we left the Hoffbrau Haus, they invited us to a nightclub called the 'Kaeffig'. Since we had never been there, we accepted their invitation. It was very nice and they had a three-man combo so we just danced the night away. I wanted a souvenir from the club but couldn't find one so I kept the cover charge stub and a wineglass. We became friendly with the musicians and promised to come back again. We were traveling by streetcar since it was so hard to get a parking place downtown and also better than having to drive after we'd had a few drinks. Well, the future brewmeisters from Argentina had a rental car so they offered to chauffeur us. As we got to the car we found a parking ticket on the windshield so all six of us pitched in to pay for it. It was well after midnight when we arrived at the police station to pay the fine. They took our money and we returned to the car only to find another parking ticket on the windshield. We were all stunned that this could happen twice in one night so we went back inside and tried to get it fixed. The policeman was very understanding and told us to go on home. So we did.

Carlos and Pedro came to our house the next day to say good-bye. Their business was over in Munich and they were taking the knowledge of making beer back home to Argentina. We stayed in contact with them by mail for a few years and they always invited us down there to visit although we never did make it.

One time Charline had company from Massachusetts, her former landlady Merrill. She wanted to see a lot of places in Europe in only four weeks time. We had a lot of Special Services Tours, but not as many as she would have liked. I started talking about Holland and the tulips and all the other countries close by and I came up with the idea that if my husband didn't mind, the three of us could go see them by car and I would drive. So we went to ask Carl. He asked how much money I would need when Merrill piped up and said that it wouldn't cost me a dime. She would pay for the gasoline, food and hotel. With that, Carl gave his approval and we started out the following day. Charline had made the trip before so she was our guide. We stayed in Holland for three nights where they have gorgeous tulip fields, windmills, and the dikes. We took a boat ride on the canal through Amsterdam and it was fascinating to see how every house was built differently. We went to the Koekenhoff, which is like a park for people to walk through, and admired the art of flowerbeds with all the colors. Another attraction was a room completely papered with cigar wrappers. No telling how many wrappers it took to cover all four walls.

Next we traveled on to Belgium. We stayed in Antwerp where we saw how a diamond is clived, also how they make lace. From there we went to Paris. We got theater tickets from Special Services to see The Folies Bergere, a most famous and beautiful revue of dances and costumes. We also visited the Eiffel Tower, the Arch of Triumph and traveled in a glass-bottomed boat on the River Seine. We were there for three days and the car battery went dead so we had to buy a new one.

Our next stop was the Riviera where we stayed in Cannes and Nice, Italy. We went to Monaco and saw Grace Kelly's Castle and also saw Monte Carlo, the gambling capital of the Riviera. We didn't go inside the casino as they wanted a hundred dollars in cover charge, but it was nice to see it from the outside. In Monaco, we also saw the changing of the guards and took pictures of the castle and it's guards. We were told that if the Princess had not been there we could have toured the inside but she was in residence at the time. We stayed at a hotel in Cannes that was so high you could touch the top of the palm trees from our balcony. We noticed that the higher the sun got the bluer the water of the Mediterranean Sea turned. We didn't go swimming in it but we did go wading and relaxed in the sand. As we traveled through Nice we had a flat tire while going down a winding road. There was just enough room to pull over, but we didn't know how to change a tire. A very nice man took pity on us and changed it for us so we gave him three packs of American cigarettes. He really liked that.

From there we traveled on to Florence, Italy. We were in awe at some of the very expensive artwork by famous painters that we got to view. We also drove through the tip of Switzerland and on to Innsbruck, Austria. We saw the famous Golden Roof there, which is made of solid gold. The story is told that during the war it was kept hidden so it wouldn't be damaged.

We also traveled to Chimsee in Germany, which is a resort for the American service men and their families. I brought back a bottle of beer for Carl from each country we visited and sent postcards faithfully. We traveled thirteen days and drove thirty-three hundred miles. When Merrill left for the states she thanked us a hundred times, at least. If it hadn't been for us she would have never seen so much of Europe.

Carl and I decided to take a family trip to Venice, Italy for a short vacation. We had planned on it for a long time and were looking forward to the trip. One morning before our departure, I woke up and my right wrist was all swollen and really hurting. I went to the doctor and he took x-rays. They revealed a fracture. I still don't know how I did it because when I went to bed that night I was fine. The only thing I can think of is that I vaguely remember my pillow had slipped between the wall and mattress and I tried to pull it out but it was wedged so tight. I thought I was dreaming but obviously I wasn't. The doctor put a short cast on my wrist that I had to wear for six weeks. What a miserable time that was but it didn't discourage me from going to Venice. The only problem was that Carl would have to do all the driving.

We really enjoyed the vacation. A favorite tourist attraction in Venice is to go on a gondola ride. I was looking forward to that but found that most of them had outboard motors on them. We wanted the real thing so we searched until we found one. The gondolier took us everywhere and showed us the highlights of the waterways.

We later stopped at a glass-blowing shop which is also very famous in this City of Amour. The glass blower made a little deer for me as a souvenir of his artwork. We also got to feed the pigeons in the square. I had never in my life seen so many hungry birds. I once heard that Venice was one of the Seven Wonders of the World. Well, maybe yes and maybe no. But I would have to concur because we did have a marvelous time even with the cast on my wrist.

I have many memories of that tour in Germany. Carl, Millie and I made many driving trips to the countryside. One day we road out to the edge of some dense woods, which Germany is famous for. It looked like it was going to rain. We saw some farmers putting bales of hay on their horse drawn wagon and it appeared as if they really needed some help so we got out and pitched in. In appreciation they invited us back to their house and we were served the most delicious afternoon snack. We had bauernbrot, a homemade rye bread, salami and smoked speck, and they offered us a glass of wine or schnapps. Of course Carl drank their 'high powered medicine' as they called it. It was a clear drink made from barley or plums and as the old saying goes, 'it's good for what ails you'. Very, very strong stuff.

On another trip to the same area we found a raspberry patch. This was my forte. I made so many goodies from the raspberries we picked, liked jelly and juice. They were equally as good when eaten plain, too. My mother had some bushes and that's where Millie learned to like them so much.

Another highlight of my time in Germany was becoming a Red Cross Volunteer, which I had always wanted to do. I signed up and took my training in Munich. After I qualified I started working in the American hospital. I was working primarily in the recreation section entertaining the patients who were able to leave their ward. We played bingo, with me as the caller. We had the old type of bingo machine where you had to pick each numbered ball from the basket and turn the basket by hand. We had some very good bingo prizes and the soldiers were happy when they could play. We also played canasta and pinochle. Some of these games could get pretty exciting. If we started a game in the afternoon and didn't finish before medication or suppertime, I would come back in the evening and we would play until the lights went out. It made me feel good to help the patients forget their illnesses for a little while. I know many of them appreciated me being there. They told me that it helped so much to do something while they were on the mend.

We still had not had our capping ceremony and the Red Cross moved up the date before I had to leave so I could get my certificate. They said it was done for me because I had the most volunteer hours out of the whole bunch that I graduated with. I was sure proud to be a regular Red Cross volunteer and will always remember our creed, "No matter what race or color, you must render your services to whoever needs them." It always made me feel good when I was able to help others.

While in Germany, Mama Millie passed away. Carl went back to North Carolina to attend the funeral by himself.

Before we had to leave Germany I saw Mama and Walter as often as possible. Leaving those two was always so hard. It broke my heart because one never knows what the future has in store for any of us and there might never be another hug or kiss from the ones you love the most.

We left Germany and came back to Fort Hood, Texas. Carl got his orders changed from Fort Dix, New Jersey to Texas at the Pentagon. Since we had a home in Texas, we naturally wanted to go back there.

NINE

Millie was now in her junior year of High School, and most of her friends were still around. It was a real homecoming for her and she graduated the following year.

Once again we had to travel to North Carolina. This time it was to attend the funeral of Carl's dad, who passed away unexpectedly. It was very sad. Now both of my in-laws were gone. I missed them greatly because they thought so much of me and loved me like a daughter.

Carl retired from the Army with a medical discharge. All the drinking he had done during his lifetime took it's toll and plagued him with cirrhosis of the liver, along with other ailments. He was in and out of the hospital. One time he had to stay at the VA hospital for four months. He came home for awhile then back to the hospital again. He really suffered a great deal. The last time he entered the hospital he lapsed into a coma for three days. His life ended on November 25th, Thanksgiving Day. He was buried in the National Cemetery at Fort Sam Houston in San Antonio. He had been a soldier for thirty-four years and he belonged with his fellow comrades. He had a twenty-one gun salute and his coffin was draped with the American flag that I received following the internment. I later gave it to the VA where it's flown every Memorial Day.

It was difficult to find a decent, good paying job and since I had no formal education here in the States, it was doubly hard. I applied for a job at the Post Exchange on Fort Hood. I had to take a test and passed with flying colors. I got the job and was pretty proud of myself. I was hired as a part-time cashier for the central check out. I still had time to do volunteer work one day a week for the Red Cross, too. I liked my job and it was fun to be among other people. My cashiering job was good until payday or when the holidays came around. You really earned your money then. The P.X. stayed busy on those days and my feet killed me from standing up all day, but when I got my paycheck it was all worth it. I loved my volunteer work, too. I was assigned to the outpatient clinic because Darnall was a new hospital and they didn't have any recreation facilities as yet. So I just stayed at the outpatient clinic and was I ever needed! I remember when we had the award ceremony and I got my first bar. We had a candlelight ceremony and General Haines passed out the awards. It was very moving realizing how much they appreciated our volunteer work and I was very happy to be a part of the team. When I made full-time cashier, however, I had to give up my volunteer work because I was working five days a week and there just was no time for anything else.

Mama had written me that Walter was getting married. I thought that was great because he had a good future and would now have a wife to support. He had a very good job working in a Volkswagen Auto firm. Everything was going well for him it seemed. Walter and his wife, Risella, had three children over the years, two girls and a boy, and it seemed as though they were very happy. I never got to meet Risella or the children because I could never afford the plane fare to Austria.

One year before Carl passed away, Millie also got married. I always dreamed she would have a beautiful wedding but it didn't happen that way. Millie and Rocky were married by a Justice of the Peace on the 2nd of December. I cried for a whole week, but it seemed she was happy and eventually the pain and my disappointment got easier. It was hurting me more not to talk to her, so we made peace with each other.

Rocky worked very hard providing a living for them. He was in the construction field. That in itself is hard work and he eventually looked for a different job. Through a friend he got a job delivering dairy products to stores. He was on the road a lot but the pay was better. Millie had gone to college for one year and then started working for Civil Service as a secretary at Fort Hood.

Mama wrote to me and said that not everything was coming up roses for Walter and his wife. Although they had the three children they filed for a divorce. That really was heart breaking for Walter and he started drinking. He loved his children, but no matter what he did it just wasn't enough for Risella. Walter turned more and more to the bottle for help, which eventually cost him his job. I found out he was living like a gypsy.

When you think nothing else could get worse, it did. The most tragic of events happened on October 30th. My beloved mother died in her sleep. I guess she worried a lot about Walter's behavior and her little boy was just doing so poorly that it broke her heart so she went to sleep forever. She was eighty-four years old. I couldn't even go home for the funeral because my passport had expired since Carl's retirement. I would have had to get a civilian passport and that costs a lot of money.

At least I had my memories of the last time I saw my mother. I had gone to see her for her eightieth birthday. Mama and Walter took me to the airport in Vienna when it was time for me to leave. She had never seen anything so big in her life and she was like a child looking at everything. I had bought a white felt hat for the trip back to Texas. It almost looked like a cowgirl hat, only more modern. Just my luck, it flew off my head as I was boarding the plane. It was very windy that day and it flew so high I thought I had lost it for sure and would never see it again. Before the doors closed for take-off the pilot brought my hat to me and told me that someone had retrieved it. Even though there were smudges on it from it's flight off my head I was glad to get it back. Through the windows of the plane I could see Mama's smiling face as she waved goodbye. That smile will stay in my heart forever to remind me always that my mother was the best.

I didn't hear from Walter for a long time after her death. Although I wrote many letters of encouragement to him they were never answered. I think more than a year had passed when I finally received a letter from him. It was a very sad letter but at least it was a sign that he was still alive. He wasn't doing well, still living like a bum and hardly eating. I worried a lot about him. Somehow my prayers for him were answered to some extent because his next letter revealed that he had slowed down on his drinking and had gotten a job. He was trying to get a grip on his life again.

Millie had worked for nine months at her job on Fort Hood when she found out she was pregnant. I was so happy that I was going to be a grandmother. On June 27th Millie presented me with a beautiful and healthy grandson. That little boy made a big difference in my life and I could have shouted from the roof tops, "I'M A GRANDMOTHER!" Millie and Rocky named him Lee. Millie didn't go back to work as she wanted to take care of her new bundle of joy. Then four years later to the day, Millie again presented me with another beautiful and healthy grandson. Both boys born on June 27th was hard to believe. They named the second addition Dean. He was a perfect little boy just like his brother, Lee. I thanked God many times for the blessings of giving me two happy, healthy grandsons.

Life was good for everyone. Millie, Rocky and the boys were doing well and it seemed Walter was doing better, too. I had a lot to be thankful for even though I was tired all the time from working. With this in mind I thought I was due to take a vacation.

When I mentioned this to my boss and friend, Elisa, she agreed that I needed a break. We thought maybe together we could go away and do something special like having some fun in Acapulco, Mexico. We checked into it and the plane fares were very good, so Acapulco it was.

Soon we were on our way to a great vacation for one whole week. We had reservations at the El Presidente, one of the better hotels. When we arrived we got a welcome cocktail of tequila and orange juice. Neither one of us drank, but we tried it anyway. Not bad at all. Our room was on the twelfth floor facing Acapulco Bay, which was a captivating scene of beauty. Many times we sat on the balcony just basking in the sunshine and relaxing. We also spent a lot of time sun bathing on the sandy beaches and enjoyed more of those 'welcome' cocktails that were served in pineapples.

We'd been there for two days and done a lot of sightseeing and shopping. We had a hard time with their money, the peso, so we had to be very careful not to go over our budget.

The following day Elisa and I were sitting under a straw umbrella sun bathing, without a care in the world, just day dreaming. A boat pulled up and two very good looking senore's came up to us and began to strike up a conversation. They spoke English very well and asked us if we could water ski. When we replied that we couldn't, they said they were willing to teach us, so we agreed to give it a try. My teachers' name was Alfredo and Elisa's was Juan. We put on life jackets and pink water skis. Alfredo put his arm around my waist in an effort to help me to stand up. I got so tickled because I felt like I was dead weight even though I only weighed a hundred and ten pounds. With the help of Alfredo I finally stood up and held on to the rope. Juan steered the boat as Elisa took pictures to show the folks back home that we really could water ski. We did pretty well. I was amazed that I could do it at all, as was Elisa. Alfredo and Juan then took us for a ride across Acapulco Bay. We stopped on the other side and enjoyed a bottle of cola. I wanted to get a nice tan, but my skin is very fair and I always blistered so Alfredo got a bottle of coconut oil and put it on me. That did the trick because I did get a tan and didn't blister at all.

That evening they took us to see the cliff divers at the El Miradore Café. We had wonderful seats right in front and it was intriguing to see the diver climb up the steep cliffs. Once he was on the top he knelt down to say a prayer then he jumped into the high tide waves. We were told the tide had to be in for the water to be deep enough. Later they took us to see Flamenco dancers. What colorful dresses they wore with every movement and step executed perfectly. It was very impressive and we had a wonderful time.

During our trip, Elisa and I took a four-hour tour on Acapulco Bay. They even had a make believe pirate on the boat so we had pictures taken with him for a souvenir. The boat turned around and as we neared the pier we saw children swimming by. As we tossed coins into the water they would dive for them. We also visited a coconut plantation where we were shown how they harvest the coconuts. After that we went on a donkey ride. The last day we had dinner at a place called the Challet where they had a three-man combo. They played my favorite song, 'La Paloma'. On our shopping expeditions we bought mini dresses and I bought maracas. We sure didn't want to leave because we really did have a wonderful time in Acapulco.

While I was working at the Post Exchange I met Roland who was a postmaster. After Carl died he helped me a great deal and became a wonderful friend to Millie and me. He even baked Lee's first birthday cake. It sure was pretty and tasted delicious. He helped out around the house and if anything needed to be repaired, he did it.

Roland also took me out to dinner and we took little trips out in the country. He was a kind and wonderful person. One day he approached me at work and said that when he got off he would stop by my house because he wanted to show me something he thought I would like to see. He came over at 7:00 p.m. and we started driving in the country. It was just before Christmas and he stopped at a little country church. They had a nativity scene outside and you could walk around the church, following the star and hear Christmas music playing. It was so touching and everything looked so real. It seemed like the Christmas spirit was right there with you.

Roland was good for my morale and he was always doing nice things for me. I remember when my brother was visiting from Canada we had a real Texas barbecue and I invited all my neighbors. Everyone brought something and I supplied the steaks and drinks. Roland made those steaks taste so good and tender that everyone complimented him. One Valentine's Day he put a heart shaped box of chocolates under my cash register and every once in a while I would find a beautiful rose. He told me one time that he loved doing things for me because I appreciated it so much. I didn't know what his marital status was at the time. I thought he was separated from his wife and getting a divorce, but we never talked about it. He started building me a brick wall for my patio and it looked so pretty, like latticework. He used white bricks and worked on it a little bit every night after work. He almost didn't finish it because something out of the blue happened. I met Len. I do believe that Roland and I would have gotten together if things had been different. He was ten years older than me but very caring as he proved to me so often.

Not so very long ago, I came across some photographs that were taken at least twenty-six years ago of Roland and me. I always had this lingering curiosity about what ever happened to him. Was he still living? Had he passed away?

I was at Millie's one Sunday afternoon and as I was walking home I noticed a strange car parked in my driveway. I couldn't believe my eyes! It was Roland! He had aged a lot, but still had that special twinkle in his eyes. He jumped out of the car and hugged me so hard I thought he was going to crush my ribs. We sat on the patio for the longest time and reminisced about the good old days. We shared some really happy memories. It had been exactly twenty-seven years since we had seen each other. He told me that he was passing through town and wondered if I still lived here, so he decided to find out. I must say it was a real surprise to see him alive and kicking. After all, he was much older than I. He told me that he was separated from his wife when I knew him way back when, but since I met and became involved with Len, he and his wife reconciled. About a year prior to this encounter, she had passed away. Before he left, he asked if I would have dinner with him from time to time. I gladly accepted, reminding him just to give me a call. Well, he did. We had a very enjoyable dinner, but he scared me to death with his driving. Maybe because I hadn't dated in such a long time. I wasn't used to someone else at the wheel. At any rate, we made it home safe and sound. He asked if he could come again for other visits and of course, I assured him that would be fine. After all, we had been good friends for so many years and I had never forgotten his kindness when Carl died. For the past two years, he comes by at Christmas and we just ride around and look at the beautiful decorations and lights that adorn the houses in our town. It always brings back such warm memories of our past.

TEN

Len entered my life quite unexpectedly. He was a very handsome divorced man who was still in the Army, but due to retire soon. He was a sergeant with the military police on Fort Hood. He was crazy about me and the first time we met he asked me to marry him. He was four years younger than I, but we enjoyed each others company tremendously. I sure wasn't ready to get married but I liked him and perhaps even fell in love with him the first time I saw him, too.

I had my vacation already planned. I was going to Austria for six weeks to see my mother for her eightieth birthday. Trusting Len, I asked if he would mind looking after my house. I told him he could even live there. I told Millie and she agreed, so he moved in. He took me to the airport and faithfully wrote to me every day while I was gone. He did a lot of repairs on the house and even built a nice cabinet for the kitchen. When I returned he flew to Dallas to meet me because he said he couldn't wait to see me. When we got to the house there was a dozen long stemmed red roses awaiting me. I had gotten roses before, but not a dozen of them. I was thrilled and so very happy.

Roland found out that I was back from overseas and stopped by the house. When he saw Len there he got pretty upset. He bowed out gracefully though, and wished me happiness. I never knew what happened to him after that.

After Len retired from the Army he started going to school at our local college. He was really smart and did well. He even talked me into taking a few courses. I had to take an aptitude test since I had not gone to school in America and had no proof that I had gone to Business College in Austria. The College over there had been bombed during the war and all the records were destroyed. I passed the exam with flying colors! In fact, the counselor who gave me the test put a letter in my file saying that I was highly qualified college material. I still worked at the PX and was made head cashier over the central checkouts. I was making more money but I still wanted to better myself. I had taken the Civil Service test before but these tests were all timed and I could not comprehend the words in the limited amount allotted.

Len was everything a woman could ask for. Although he went to college he still found time to have supper ready when I got home from work. He was a real Betty Crocker when it came to the kitchen!

I finally quit my job and went to college full-time. The first semester I had three different English's and a Business Math class. I did real well but boy was I ever nervous! I felt like a little girl attending school for the first time in her life. To my surprise I did better than I thought. I passed all my subjects and was ready for the second semester.

Before second semester started Len and I went to Canada to visit my brother Johnny. I had been to Canada twice before to visit him but Len had never been there. Johnny had always invited us but the time never permitted us to go until now.

We had a wonderful flight and Johnny and his landlady, Madge, who was like a mother to him, picked us up at the airport. Madge would always say that Johnny had been with her longer than he was with his own mother. She really loved him. Madge had two daughters, Lena and

Beth. Both of them were married to millionaires. Johnny had lived at their mother's house for the last forty years and Lena and Beth thought of him as their little brother.

Madge was so happy that she finally had gotten to meet Len and she liked him instantly. Beth and her husband Bill invited us all for dinner and we had a wonderful meal served with wine and all the amenities. Beth is a very good cook and it was really amazing. Although they were very rich they really treated us like they were just everyday people.

The next day Lena and her husband, Phil, invited us to the Ponderosa Restaurant, which was excellent. Then off we went to their country club. What a fancy place that was. We took the grand tour, had a drink then left. Johnny took Len fishing one day but they didn't catch anything. They had a great time anyway. While we were there Johnny showed us the plane he flew when he was a Bush Pilot and also took us on a boat ride through the Soo Locks all of which was very interesting. He showed us all around his city of Sault St. Marie. Canada was so much like Europe. Although they speak English, the stores carry a lot of European merchandise. I brought back some goodies like candy that we didn't have in Texas. I also bought some lottery tickets. Later when Johnny sent me the winning numbers, I was only one number off. To think, I could have been a millionaire, too.

I love the way they take care of their lawns in Canada. Everything is so green but, of course, the weather never gets as hot up there as it does in Texas. It really was a very pleasant trip and everybody was so wonderful to us. We had to promise that we would be back again for another visit one day.

I did go back several years later but it was not a happy event. It was to my brother's funeral. Johnny died of bone cancer after suffering nearly a year with that deadly disease. He was buried in the same grave as Madge's husband, because she always said he was like the son she never had. He never married but was in love at one time with a nurse. She died in an automobile accident and Johnny never found love again. I'm just so glad Madge and her family were there for him for all those years. Madge is gone now too, she was ninety-four years old when she died of heart failure. Lena and Beth took me in as their sister and we have kept in touch over the years, always signing off with 'Love, Sis'. I look at my many pictures of all of us, which always reminds me of that fantastic visit Len and I took to Canada.

I took the Civil Service test again and passed, but with a low score. I took it over and over since you could take it every six weeks and each time my score would get a little higher. I continued college for the second semester and took part two of English and also typing and business machines. I was trying to get my associates degree. I also took photography, business management and History I and II. I made good grades, but I still put in for a Civil Service job. I was interviewed for a cashier's position in the Commissary and got the job. Mrs. Selma, my boss, said she thought I would make a good cashier because I knew how to handle the public, which is of great importance.

I loved my new job and it was so much easier than the PX. There I had forty-two cashiers to oversee. It was a big responsibility for such a small paycheck. Here I was only accountable for only my own money till. We had a contest among the cashiers to see if we could make ten thousand dollars in one eight-hour day. Whoever won would get an award. Well, you guessed it; yours truly got the grand prize. I also made Employee of the Month, which was really a great honor, since your peers and fellow employees chose you.

I had a lot of friends in the commissary but there was one very special friend and every time he walked by my register he would say something funny to lift my spirits. This was especially nice when we were so very busy. I recall one time when he brought me a small token of his affection. He opened his jacket and said, "I'm giving you my heart." With that he pulled out a tiny fuzzy heart. He sure embarrassed me but it wouldn't be the first or last time. On another occasion he was talking to me and a customer walked up. He told her we were getting married and she asked if she could arrange the reception. From then on we became very famous because people believed him. He did so many funny and nice things, too. I came to work one morning and as I reached for my time card there was a rose clipped to it. Nobody knew who had done it but later he confessed. My dear friend, Anselmo. It was a wonderful gesture. Many times he would call me at home. He lived in a neighboring city and the railroad ran near his house. Sometimes we would talk as long as it took for the train to come from there to my town and then say goodnight.

There has never been anything between us except friendship but you would think by his behavior that he had a major crush on me. Many times when he would say we are getting married, customers would comment on what a handsome couple we made.

In 1986, Anselmo again proved to be a good friend when I had a tragic accident. One Sunday I was overwhelmed with an abundance of energy. It was a beautiful day, and also my day off from work. On my daughter's house right next door there was a turbo vent installed on the roof. The wind had been blowing very hard and the axle was flown off. It was making some terrible screeching noises as it turned and, being by myself for so long, I had learned a lot of these 'Mr. Fix-It' trades. It was at this point that I decided to put the vent back on the axle. How hard could it possibly be? I dragged my aluminum extension ladder next door and leaned it up against the house. At one time, years before, there had been a shed sitting on a cement slab, but not being anchored down very well high winds eventually blew it over. My daughter had the metal removed, but the frame cemented into the slab was still there. I began the climb up the ladder. I had only two more rungs before reaching the roof, as the ladder began to slip and I fell down onto the cement slab. When Millie heard my screams she came running to the back door. At that point, she, too, began screaming for someone to please call an ambulance. Millie saw the blood gushing from my head and kept encouraging me to hang in there, that help was on the way. In no time the paramedics arrived, but I kept slipping in and out of consciousness. I do remember a man bending over me before the ambulance arrived. A black man with the kindest eyes, he tirelessly comforted me. With the arrival of the ambulance and the police, they worked feverishly to stabilize me. I don't remember very much because my mind was getting foggier and foggier. From what little I do recollect, only in bits and pieces, I was put on a board and taken to the emergency room at Fort Hood. I was x-rayed from top to bottom checking for any broken bones. It was very apparent to me that I did have a broken wrist, because it was facing backwards. There was also a large gash on the top of my head. After four long hours in the x-ray and examining room came the real shocker! The emergency room doctors informed me that I had a compression fracture in my back, lumbar number four. I also had a broken right wrist, a fracture of the left wrist at the base of my index finger and a concussion, which explained the dizziness I was experiencing. Needless to say, I was admitted to the hospital. The doctors told me I was fortunate to have survived the fall. Then came the ultimate blow. I was told I had a broken back. At this point I wasn't sure whether or not I really wanted to go on living.

Being from Austria, music had always played a big role in my life. If I couldn't dance any more and enjoy life to the fullest, my existence was of no meaning anymore. Before taking me to my room the doctors had to close my head with sixteen stitches and put both my hands in casts. The pain I felt from the injuries was more than I could endure. Even though I was on pain medication it didn't seem to help, perhaps because at this point I had no will to live.

I will never forget when Millie called the Chaplain to come pray with me. When he arrived, we talked and prayed. Soon the medications began working; or else the divine power of God helped me find peace. Finally I dozed off. When I awoke the following morning my whole attitude had changed. Even though I still had a lot of pain, the will to live again had resurfaced. It was at this point that I made up my mind. I was going to conquer this and get better with every breath I took! Now I was fighting to survive for Millie and my grandsons. There were many unpleasant hours. With both of my arms in casts, I was helpless. I had to wait until the nurses or somebody could come to spoon feed me. For the first time in my life, I was totally dependent on someone else. The nurses, my dearest Millie and friends were so wonderful to me. I was fitted with a back support brace, and after eight days of lying on my back, I was permitted to sit in a chair for ten minutes. Then came the process of learning how to walk again. If that wasn't bad enough I'd developed yet another problem. I couldn't go to the bathroom! I was given all kinds of stool softeners, but nothing worked. The miracle came on the tenth day! I had a male nurse, a lieutenant, who really took excellent care of me and was very concerned about my problem. When he heard that I had finally made progress, he called me on the intercom over my bed with the announcement "Congratulations, Monika! It was a ten pound baby boy!" Happy as I was, I was still a little embarrassed by his comment.

Soon came the time for my therapy. I had to start walking three times a day, from my bed to the nurse's station. Each day I became stronger and my bones began to mend slowly but surely. On the seventeenth day of my hospital stay I received the best news! I could go home. Since I lived alone, I was a little anxious. How was I supposed to put on my brace when both of my arms were in casts? The hospital commander gave approval for a nurse to come to my house and help me. Millie was talking to one of the teachers at the school where she works about me, and her concerns for my well being. The teacher told Millie that her mother was in town and would be happy to help out and stay with me until Millie got home from work. It would really be therapeutic for her as well by breaking up her monotonous days. Mary, which was the lady's name, was very kind and good-hearted. What a blessing it was that she came into my life. I will always be grateful to her for her patience and concern.

Gradually things began to improve for me. Finally one cast was removed, so at least now I could wash my face alone. To me this was some enormous accomplishment! I was off from work for three months, and when I did go back it was only light duty. There was another friend, a Mexican lady named Bonita, who made sure I always had something to eat. When I think of the many people that were there for me, when I was so desperately in need, I feel truly blessed. Words can never express my gratitude to Millie, Anselmo and the many friends who helped me get back on my feet again. I never did find out who the black man with the kind eyes was. My neighbor said he was just walking down the street and jumped over the fence to help.

My bones have mended well. They say everyone has a Guardian Angel. Well, I do believe in miracles and my Guardian Angel was truly looking out for me. Every year when the fourth of March comes around, I kneel down and thank God for sparing my life!

Later on things ended between Anselmo and and me because he got a different job. I really missed him. He would call sometimes but the calls became further apart. Sometimes as much as six months would go by. He had given me his phone number but I never called. I have no idea what happened to him. Perhaps he really did get married.

Many years went by and one day, out of the blue, he called and asked if he could see me. I was delighted. We talked for a long time and reminisced of old times. He started calling me more often and coming by the house too, but the big shocker came on my birthday. He sent me a dozen long stemmed roses. I wasn't home when the delivery came, but he told the florist if that should happen to take them next door to Millie's house. I was so surprised and also very happy when I saw them. He had never done that before, but his true friendship made it one of the nicest birthdays I ever had. He doesn't come over too often now but he does call or send emails. We have been friends for about seventeen years now and the good Lord willing we will remain friends for a lifetime.

Now, back to my college days and Len. When I started working full time I had to give up going to school. There just wasn't time. I could have taken night classes but not being a night person I didn't think I could handle that. I decided that when I retired I would have plenty of time to get my degree.

I was never happier than when I was with Len. We lived together for nine and a half years and I loved him with all my heart. Finally I agreed to marry him. We decided to get married in Las Vegas with my friends El and Walt as our witnesses. We planned the trip for May 30th. We had our plane tickets and hotel reservations plus everything else required making it legal to become husband and wife. We wanted to surprise all our friends when we came back from vacation, but it wasn't meant to be. Len wasn't feeling well so he went to the doctor. The doctor said he was congested but the medication should help him. We still had two weeks to go before we left for our trip. He seemed to be feeling better and we were looking forward to it and ready to go. On May 23rd, Len had a massive heart attack and died. I will never forget that night. All the happiness I'd had in the last nine years, with more to look forward to in the future would never come to pass. It was erased in the seven hours he lived after the heart attack. I buried him at Fort Sam Houston National Cemetery. He was a soldier and fought the wars. He belonged there.

When I visit the graves of both Carl and Len, I am always grateful that I had known love twice in my lifetime. I loved Carl very much, but I was so young. Then I found love again when I was a mature adult.

I had been retired for perhaps a year and was visiting my neighbor, Ilsa. She had mentioned that her son who lived in Indiana wanted her to come and visit him, but she didn't want to drive that far by herself. I had just bought a new car, a Buick La Sabre, and it really should be taken on the road to break it in. I told her that I hadn't been traveling to other states in quite a while, and thought it would be a real treat for us to go visit her son, Garrett. The more we thought about it, the more anxious we were to get on the way. Ilsa was also a widow who had lost her husband several year prior. Thankfully, she knew the roads since her husband was from Ohio and they had made the trip many times. We mapped out our route, packed our luggage and left the following week. We started out bright and early. The sun was glistening and we were feeling great. We stopped in Bossier City, Louisiana, for gasoline and lunch. Of course, we also gambled for about an hour, then we were on our way again. So far, I had really enjoyed it. I'd always loved to travel and since it had been quite a while it was a double treat. Having so much in common with Ilsa was a plus as well. She was from Germany, had married a soldier and been my neighbor for years.

We bought our houses about the same time, and rented them out when we got orders elsewhere. We always came back to the old homestead. We were just approaching Hope, Arkansas. I had never been there, but it was nice to visit considering our current President hailed from the small town. We, thus far, had been making really good time and the car was running just as smooth as could be. When I would get tired of driving, Ilsa would take over. We spent the night in Missouri, and after breakfast we hit the road again. As we drove through Illinois, I took a picture as we crossed the bridge entering into the state. We called Garrett to let him know that we would be arriving the following day.

We arrived at Garrett's home around four in the afternoon. It was sure nice to get to our destination after such a long drive. Garrett was very happy to see us and although we were exhausted, we stayed up half the night talking. I had watched as Garrett grew up and since he had attended school with Millie we had some catching up to do. We finally called it a day around two in the morning.

Garrett showed us all the surrounding places and highlights. We went to a winery, a famous park, and for the first time in my life I saw a clan of Amish people. (The locals called them the horse and buggy people.) We stopped in a store and bought a cookbook called "Cooking with the Horse and Buggy People". It truly had some intriguing recipes. Our next tour was to a mill that ground corn into corn meal, run by the

Amish. Then we watched with great interest the weavers who allowed me to photograph them. The next adventure was on the Gambling Riverboat. Naturally, we just had to try our luck. Although we had been lucky in having a safe trip, our luck ran out when it came to gambling. It set us back about two hundred dollars. We didn't stay there too long!

All too soon it was time to say good-bye and off we went. This time our route took us through Kentucky where we stopped at Loretta Lynn's mansion where she and Mooney had spent so many years before he passed away. We enjoyed a wonderful dinner at one of her restaurants with some real southern cooking. Leaving Kentucky, we went through Tennessee, back to Missouri, Arkansas, Louisiana and finally Texas. We had a free room in Bossier City at one of the Casinos, so we took advantage of it. Thankfully, we were a little luckier and got some of our money back. After a restful night, we finally made it home. I unpacked all my souvenirs; the bottle of wine that Garrett had bought me at the winery, the Amish cookbook and, of course, the many photos we had taken. Every one came out just perfect with the exception of one. When I bought the cookbook, I asked if I could take a picture of the lady who sold it to me. She agreed, but when they were developed I discovered I'd shot the ceiling. From her face down to her waist all was a blur. Her skirt, apron and counter came out perfectly, though. I've heard that the Amish don't want their pictures taken. I guess this was proof that the story was true. I showed the snapshots to Ilsa who thought it was also strange. I will always remember our trip and the many sights we viewed. As for my car, it was doing well too! She proved she was great on long distances and extremely good on gasoline.

ELEVEN

It didn't take long to discover just how much time I had on my hands after my retirement, a condition I was certainly not accustomed to. I managed, though, to busy myself. Besides traveling and playing bingo, I went window shopping, always looking for the best bargains.

One day I entered an arts and crafts shop that was going out of business. I bought some odds and ends that I really thought I could use when I felt like doing handcrafts. I came across eight panels of material that could be embroidered and since I enjoy doing things like that, I bought it, not having a clue what I was going to use it for. One day I began to embroider the panels. I made all the flowers in French knots, which gave it an embossed look, then just set it aside.

Weeks had gone by and I never thought about the beautiful work I had begun, even though I had put a lot of love and time into it. My neighbor, Caroline, enjoyed making quilts. All of hers were prize-winning, one more beautiful than the next. We were talking one day over a cup of coffee and I mentioned that I wished I could do that. With that comment, she offered to help. Two days later I had a dream that I could use these beautiful embroidered panels that I had set aside on a quilt. I mentioned this to Caroline, who thought it just might be a good idea. She showed me how to cut the material that I had purchased to fill in the panels. It was time consuming, but slowly my quilt started to look better and better. Finally, the top was finished. I had to buy some batting and also a bottom sheet. We pinned it on a quilting frame and prepared for the hard work that was to come.

Hand-quilting little stitches at a time, I sure wish I had a penny for every prick my fingers got. It took me about two months before the quilt was completed. In our town we had a quilting show coming up and every one who saw it urged me to enter my work. I was really debating this because I could see some of my mistakes. My dear Millie finally convinced me, remarking on how beautiful it was and that I should really show it off. With her encouragement and that of neighbors and friends, I finally relented. When my quilt was in the showroom hanging on the wall, I truly thought it was the most interesting and gorgeous one in the whole show. I was so proud of it! I'd put my whole heart and soul into creating it. During the time that I was working on my quilt, Millie remarked that this would be an heirloom, passed down from generation to generation. We returned to the show the following day to view the comments of the judges. Three judges critiqued mine with comments like 'most beautiful color combination' and 'most interesting lay out', but it was sagging at the edges. I must have pulled the material when I was sewing the edging on. It really didn't matter, though. I was so proud of what the judges had said about the first quilt I had ever made.

Now I display my accomplishment in my spare bedroom, to be admired by the company that visits me. I will always be grateful to my dear neighbor, Caroline, who encouraged me and helped to make it. Friends have asked me if I will ever make another one. My reply remains the same. Perhaps one day when I get old and have nothing else to do I will try my hand at it again. For now, however, I still have a lot of traveling and sight seeing to do. I want to visit all the people that I love the most, too, my sweet little great-granddaughter, Krystine, my wonderful, handsome grandsons, Krystine's mama, Noelle, and so many more.

Millie is still harping on the 'heirloom factor', adamant that she will get it first and rightfully so. Then it can go down the family chain so that her mother's work of art can be shown off. I must admit that I'm very proud and happy that everyone likes it.

TWELVE

It seems that divorce runs in the family, because after ten years of marriage, Millie and Rocky called it quits. Rocky had joined the police force and just wasn't the same after that. It hurt me a lot because here was Millie with two little boys and all on her own. I think this was a turning point for me. I loved my grandsons with all my heart and now I would do everything in my power to give them all my help, my heart and my love so that they might have a good future!

A year had passed since the divorce and on December 7th, Pearl Harbor Day, I thought my life was coming to an end. Little Dean, only four years old, was riding his big wheel at his friend, Shane's house two blocks away, when a speeding car hit him as he rode down the driveway to the street. It was about six o'clock in the evening when Lee came running to my door and said, "Nannie come quickly! Dean has been hit by a car." Lee and I went running down the street. I still don't know where I got the strength to get there. I was crying and praying to the good Lord not to let him die. When Lee and I got there, Millie was watching them put Dean into an ambulance so they could rush him to the hospital. We followed by car. To this day, I can't remember how we made it.

At the hospital, the doctors said that Dean had internal injuries and they would need to operate. He had a crushed spleen, a bleeding kidney and several lacerations on his head. The surgeon had to remove the spleen and hoped the kidney would heal. So many prayers were said for that little boy pleading for a speedy recovery. With the mercy of God, He answered our prayers, and Dean's kidney started working again. Our little boy was such a fighter. When he came out of surgery his first utterance was 'Nannie'. Words cannot describe the joy, love and thanks I had in my heart. As tears rushed down my cheeks, the family came together, hugging each other with some nurses joining in. For all of us it was truly a miracle that happened just before Christmas. My sweet, innocent little grandson had survived this ordeal. He came home from the hospital just before Christmas and even though he was still weak, at least he was with us. I had a silver Christmas tree that Dean and Lee helped me decorate. We will always remember that special silver tree and how grateful we were to be able trim it together. Today, my handsome grandson, Dean, is twenty-five years old and stands six foot six. You would never know that twenty-two years ago he was so frail. He now lives in Austin, our State Capital, and has a good paying job in fiber optics.

Lee, now twenty-nine, with movie star looks, lives in Dallas where he manages a store and is doing really well. He is married and has a beautiful wife, Noelle. They bought a hundred and twenty thousand-dollar home that has a thirty-two foot long in-ground swimming pool with a waterfall at the end. I even enjoy it when I go for visits. Six years ago they made me a great-grandmother when Noelle delivered a gorgeous baby girl who is my pride and joy. Her name is Krystine and she has brought so much happiness into my life. My love for her and her love for me will last through eternity. She is not only beautiful, which she gets from her mother, but also smart, which she inherited from her father. Lee has a computer-like memory, especially when it comes to numbers. He can tell you the total of a line of numbers without any effort at all. He is also a shopaholic, always looking for the best deals in everything. I have learned a lot from him and he looks out for my best interests.

My sweet Krystine calls me 'Nannie' like everyone else. I recall when she was born everyone asked what she was going to call me. Lee and Noelle both said, "Why, Nannie, of course!" This made me very happy. When she entered this world I remember saying that I hoped I would live long enough to see her start school. Well, she started kindergarten in August of 2000, so this one goal was met.

Five years ago I battled breast cancer and today I can proudly say I am a cancer survivor. This has given me a new perspective on life and I have set new goals for myself. Now I want to live long enough to be at Krystine's graduation. I have survived many obstacles in my life and I hope that with God's will, He will grant me this one last wish.

One day I got a picture postcard from Spain that was signed 'Walter and Marlene'. I was so happy to hear from him and to know that he had found a companion to enjoy life with again. More cards arrived from different countries in Europe, as well as small gift packages for Christmas and Easter, all from Walter and Marlene. I also sent gifts to them for the holidays. The last package I mailed was in December, 1999. I received a Christmas card from them letting me know that the package had arrived and that a letter would follow.

I waited and waited, but no letter came. I wrote a few more times but never received a reply. I just had a gut feeling that something was wrong. Walter sounded so happy in his letters so there should have been no reason for him not to write. I even told Millie that Walter was either dead or in jail because none of my letters had been answered. I couldn't write to Marlene because I didn't have her address. I didn't even know her last name. I also didn't know where his ex-wife and children lived. I made up my mind to write to the local police department in the city where he lived. Maybe they could help me. It's not hard to locate someone in Austria because you have to be registered where you live. If you move you must give a forwarding address.

On July 12th, 2000, I received news that tested my strength once again. I got a letter from Marlene. She informed me that my son, Walter, had died June 22nd, after a brief illness with lung cancer. She said that when they found out he had cancer, it was too late for treatments that might help. The cancer was far too advanced. After fifty-three years of balancing the scales of his persona, between happiness and sadness, his life had ended.

Marlene must have been a very kind and loving person. She laid him to rest, using her own money to pay for the funeral. I owe her so much gratitude and respect for this and am grateful for all that she did for Walter. She told me that she loved him. He brought a lot of sunshine into her life after the death of her husband who also lost his bout with cancer. She described the funeral to me and it must have been very touching. She said only two of Walter's children attended the memorial, but so many friends paid their last respects to him. Young people, as well as the old who had watched him grow up in the nearby community where his mama/grand-mother reared him and molded him into a man.

I have shed a lot of tears in the last fifty-three years, thinking of the son I had, but never really knew. I am seventy-two years old now, retired, and pray for Walter's forgiveness for the mistake I made when I was nineteen.

I remember so vividley and I'm so grateful for having had the chance to be with Walter just that one time, when I went home for my mother's 80th birthday. My son had asked me if I was interested in driving into the beautiful Alpine Mountains and perhaps even go highter up on the ski lift. I was so happy when he suggested that and we left the next morning. As we got closer to these majestic wonders, it brought back so many wonderful and so very happy memories of my early teenage years.

On weekends, some of my school friends and I would go by train then hike up some hills that weren't so high and spend one or two nights at the challet, provided by the Austrian Mountain Sociaty (Gebirgs Herbege) and almost every challet had two floors which separated the boys from the girls. They had an overseer or chaperone for each floor. After breakfast, all the boys and girls would get together and play games or go hiking to different hills. Before bed time we would sit together in the dining area and one of the counselors played the accordian and we would all sing or even yodel, well those who could, and we also told jokes which we thought were pretty good. After that we said a silent prayer and it was lights out and we all went to dreamland. When Sunday came it was time to go home since Monday was another school day. Walter and I stopped at a resturant for lunch and of course I had to have the world famous Vienna Schnitzel (breaded veal cutlet) and I even had a glass of wine. After lunch we took the ski lift, to go higher up the mountain. What a wonderful sight that was while going up. We passed some of the beautiful mountain flowers such as the delicate off white edelweis with it's tiny yellow centers, also the bell shaped blue enzian and we also saw the varigated pink almrausch. Once we were on top we truly enjoyed the pure mountain air. We were up so hight that you could reach out and almost touch the face of God. As we walked around we still could see snow in the ravines which was shaded from the sun. On our way back home we stopped at a souvenier shop and I bought one item that I still have today, a thermometer that shows the temperature both in American and European gauges. I always had trouble converting that. We also took a lot of pictures on that trip. I wanted Millie to see her half brother also the land she was born in. When I look at the photographs I still can remember that happy day when I had my son for a little while all to myself. That was also the last time I saw him.

I have invited Marlene to visit me in Texas. I really want to meet her. She accepted, so perhaps in the year 2001 she will come to visit. I am looking forward to that.

Now that everyone is gone, Papa and Mama, my brother, Johnny and now my son, Walter, the only family I have left is the one that Carl and I created. I have written this, my life story, for Millie, Lee, Dean and Krystine so that they will know and understand me a little better. Hopefully answers have been given to questions like the mystery surrounding Walter.

I live alone now, but Millie and her new husband, Tim, live right next door. Millie married Tim seven years ago and I do believe he loves her very much. He has been so good to me, as well as her boys. He is a computer whiz and helps a great number of people with their home computers. A couple of years ago, for Mothers Day, he and Millie gave me one. I was sure intimidated by it, thinking I might break something or mess it up. My dear son-in-law assured me if something should go wrong, he could fix it. At first, I just played games on it. When my eyes started burning from looking at the screen, Lee bought me a different one that really helped. I'm more confident with the computer now so here I am, typing my memoirs and getting acquainted with cyber space.

For their second wedding anniversary, I invited Tim and Millie to join me in a slot machine tournament in Las Vegas. Tim's father was flying in from Hawaii and his brother was coming in from New Jersey. It was almost like a family reunion for them. We were in Las Vegas for five fun-filled days. Since we were in the slot machine tournament, our rooms were free and the meals were compliments of the casino. We played for three days and each day was filled with excitement. We even managed to make some pretty high scores. Maybe it was because of the current music and dance craze, "The Macarena."

The theme of the tournament was "Aloha Hawaii" so it was very appropriate that the last night we were served a Hawaiian Luau of roast pig and all the fixings. It was truly wonderful. The top players were at the guest of honor table in the middle of the dining room, each table decorated with tiny orchids in exquisite vases. Now might be a good time to mention exactly who was at the winner's table. Tim, Millie and I came in as the number one team! We each received a glass plague and, of course, a check that we divided equally. Camera flashes were coming from all directions with congratulations from all.

Tim's father, better known as Big Bad John, sent Millie and me authentic Hawaiian muumuus, and needless to say, we were very proud to wear them. Big Bad John took us to a seafood restaurant one evening. The centerpiece was a carved statuette of a mermaid, which really brought out the artistic values of the sculptor. I dreaded the end of our five-day adventure, but when that day came, as we were leaving the casino, bigger than Dallas, there were our names on the Marquee! The parting was bitter sweet as Big Bad John returned to Hawaii and Tim's brother went back to New Jersey. Tim and Millie thanked me profusely for their anniversary gift, with my reminder to them not to expect such a lavish trip every year. Of course, they took it in the manner that I presented. About two weeks after our return, we received some beautiful photographs from the casino management, a reminder of our fabulous stay!

Millie is a secretary at one of our local elementary schools and works with computers everyday. She has been a great help to me and has shown me how to use the Word Perfect program. I have mastered the English language pretty well, but there are still words I need help with so I use Mr. Webster for a reference. Word Perfect, with a little practice, is just ideal for people like me.

When Millie and Tim were married, his father lived in Hawaii. For their first anniversary he invited them to visit and also invited me. He was very generous, and paid for almost everything. The trip was a dream come true for me. When I was growing up, I always dreamed of visiting Hawaii and now it had come to pass. We stayed for ten days, visiting two islands. We saw so many sights in Honolulu and even got to see a film crew shooting a movie. We visited the sugar factory where Tim's father worked. It was incredible to see how sugar was made. We saw so many things I could write a whole book on just that. I will never forget our trip to paradise.

The three men in my life, Lee, Dean and Tim are very good to me and have made my life a lot easier in my golden years. Lee has given me all sorts of timesaving gadgets. Last year he bought me a brand new lawn mower that is self-propelled. I don't know how the grass ever was mowed before I got this new one. It has a mulcher and starts with just one pull! This was a special gift because I love to work outside and it's so much easier. Dean always helps me with the big things like pruning the tree limbs. Sometimes, though, he can get carried away! I had a cedar tree in front of my house that I brought back from Alabama when it was only ten inches tall. As it grew over the years we would decorate it with Christmas lights and outdoor ornaments. It got so big, though, that it was ruining my roof so I asked Dean to cut it down…a little. I could hang some flowerpots on it. Well, I thought I heard a chain saw but didn't realize that the sound was coming from my front yard. When I looked outside, my cedar tree had been reduced to a two-foot stump. I yelled out that that was good enough. I now have a flowerpot sitting there with runners going down to the ground. It looks pretty good.

Lee stopped in for a quick visit a few months ago while seeing a friend on business. He asked how my microwave was holding up. I told him it was getting old but still working. With that, he went out to his car and brought in the biggest microwave I had ever seen. He removed the little old one and set up the new one for me. It hardly fit on the shelf. I had a time getting used to it and at first burned a few things but now I just love it and it takes half the time to cook.

Dean bought me some fancy pots and pans last year for Christmas and I got new silverware from Lee. I was so happy to replace the old ones I have had for so long. Then a couple of months ago Dean called and asked if I needed a new refrigerator. I had an old one on the patio which had to be defrosted every so often so he brought me a new one that's self-defrosting. To top things off, this past Christmas my two wonderful grandsons got together and bought me a new range. I was so surprised I just cried. The final touch to my new kitchen and equipment was the installation of new cabinets. Dean, who is so agile with his hands, put them up in no time. Believe me, I am one happy grandmother!

Tim is always there when needed too. He is a 'gadget man' and has given me several things over the years. Some I can use and some are too complicated for me, but the gifts are always given and received with love. He is also my handy man when something breaks or doesn't work right. Every year he hangs my Christmas lights outside and is definitely my helping hand.

My girls are important to me, too. When I found out that I had breast cancer, Millie was my guiding light. She was there for me one hundred percent. I don't know what I would have done without her. I will never forget and will always be deeply grateful to my dear, caring Noelle. The day of my surgery she and Krystine drove two and a half-hours to the hospital. She wanted to make sure I saw my great-granddaughter before I went into surgery. In fact, they arrived before me. She knew I was so frightened and that it would make me feel so much better. That was such a wonderful and thoughtful thing for her to do. She also stayed with me a few days after I came home, helping me bathe, picking up around the house and keeping me company. Her kindness helped me get back on my feet again.

I know in my heart that if there is a crisis in our family we are all there for each other. I am very proud of each and everyone and feel so very blessed to have them near me and to be so caring.

The time has come to end my story. There's been an awful lot of living, laughing and loving in my life and I'm truly thankful for all that has been bestowed upon me. To all those so very near and dear to my heart, let me say, "God Bless You All!"

www.ingramcontent.com/pod-product-compliance
Lightning Source LLC
Chambersburg PA
CBHW031240280526
45784CB00004B/1650